THINK RICH / LIVE RICH

"The tools to becoming the rich you"

By

Tre Nitty Gritty

Acknowledgements

I want to thank GOD, my family, friends, and supporters.

Preface

This is a book that is meant to be studied. Re read and highlight as you go through it and take in all that you can. Use this as a tool to help you get into the mindest of thinking rich and living rich.

Your mind is a powerful tool that can maifest things into reality. If you are constantly on negative thoughs, youre going to manifest tha tinto your reality. Thinking in a more positive way and manifesting the things you want will create that reality. You can use this to your advantage and live a rich life by thinking rich.

Heres some things you should do...

- Use any white space to write in notes, thoughts, feelings, etc.
- Highlight phrases or paragraphs that speak to you or make you feel empowered or could help contribute to a more positive mindset
- Theres no right or wrong way to read this book. Read at your own pace and in any order you see fit.
- Take what you need at the time from this book. Feel free to come back to this book at different times when you are needing guidance.

INTRODUCTION

First off... I would like to thank and congratulate you for taking your first step towards thinking rich and living rich by opening **THINK RICH / LIVE RICH** on a quest of obtaining the tools to become the rich you.

Think Rich, Live Rich is a formula for growth and development. Providing valuable information, universal applicable tools and strategies of conquering ourselves, inspiring and motivating others to become the masters of their thoughts and actions.

By releasing this radiant, positive energy into the universe we are exposing others to an aura that will seep into their pores and enter their nervous systems, taking over their minds, erasing all negative thoughts, providing a rich, clean and pure foundation to build upon, planting seeds of growth, determination, patience, balance, confidence, morals and principles.

I welcome you to join me on this journey of Think Rich / Live Rich for this will become a part of your everyday life.

Together we can create change.

Open doors and invite the entire world to become ONE with THINKING and LIVING rich.

So, let's take this time to Think Rich / Live Rich and begin spreading these riches.

TOOL # 1

CLEANSE THE MIND

"Solitude is a very important factor in finding peace of mind... Seclude and cleanse yourself"

Remove yourself from the world for at least ten minutes a day and meditate. Whatever it takes to bring you inner peace whether it be prayer, a hot shower, working out, going out for a jog, taking a walk, going on a drive or by simply relaxing.

The key is to get comfortable, take a deep breath, hold it for one second then release slowly.

Repeat this process over and over...

Each time that you exhale imagine that you are blowing out every bit of stress, steam, pressure and pain. Every negative thought, feeling and emotion.

Imagine yourself amongst the midst of the sweetest aroma. Your eyes are set upon the most beautiful horizon that you have ever seen. Relax your body and continue to pace your breathing.

Once you have cleansed your mind of all the clutter

IT IS TIME TO BEGIN

Thinking RICH & Living RICH

TOOL # 2

RICH SELF TALK

"WITH RICH SELF- TALK, YOU CAN TALK YOUR WAY TO SUCCESS"

You have to begin thinking successfully and speaking rich things into existence. I often hear people say that there is nothing wrong with talking to yourself and that there isn't anything for you to be worried about until you begin answering your own questions. I'd ask those same people... "What is the sense in asking yourself a question, without coming to the conclusion of an answer?" Then I would advise them to begin having =RICH SELF TALK=.

Start your day off with positive thoughts and ask yourself... "How am I going to make this day count? "Set a goal, formulate a plan to accomplish it, then execute it. Don't make excuses, make things happen. You have to constantly remind yourself that you can do anything that you put your mind to. There is a lot of truth in the saying that "If you tell yourself something so often, you'll begin to believe it."   So, make sure that you are only planting rich thoughts into your garden of thinking.

Tell yourself things like it's time to get up, get out and go get it. Your very own world is resting in the palms of your hands.... It's left up to you to do the building. Having or not having =RICH SELF TALK= could prove to be the fine line that separates you from success or failure.

TOOL # 3

BE THANKFUL

Give thanks to the blessing of waking up and having the opportunity of experiencing another day above ground. There are so many things to be thankful for, yet most of the time there is a need for training our brains and fine tuning our eyes in order for us to see them clearly.

Something as simple as taking a breath might not be appreciated as much as it should be until we experience having complications breathing correctly or having the ability to breathe on our own without the help of a machine or mechanism.

A NEAR DEATH EXPERIENCE COULD BE THE BIRTH OF A NEW AWAKENING.

Some people are born with disabilities, either that or develop them whether physically or mentally. Others lack the luxury of possessing certain functioning organs inside of their bodies, yet we choose to destroy our very own by knowingly causing damage to ourselves on a day-to-day basis from the unhealthy food that we crave and eat while ignoring our consciousness of the consequences, allowing our subconscious minds control our actions.

Putting poisonous toxins inside of our bodies in the form of Tobacco products and alcoholic beverages to drugs whether illegal or prescriptions prescribed by doctors is only a temporary fix that in turn causes permanent damage, side effects, addiction, chemical imbalances and the need for additional drugs and or medication to balance out the instabilities.

We have to be thankful for the temples that God has provided us with being that they are the vehicles that transport our spirits and no matter the dollar amount that we may be worth financially we do not have the option of purchasing another one if and when it happens to break down on us. Just because we can't see the internal damage that we are causing does not mean that it is non-existent.

Be thankful for your family if you are blessed to have one because whether or not you have noticed there are some people who do not have any family or anyone to act as family in their lives, yet these are usually some of the most grateful people in the world.

What we take for granted there are others who would cherish wholeheartedly. The less fortunate tend to appreciate the small things in life, as should we all.

Appreciate the road that you are traveling and all of the lessons that you have learned along the way. Be thankful for the wins and the losses. Everything that it has taken to get you where you are today is what builds you into a strong individual who is able to withstand the storms that you have once survived and the knowledge to deal with other unexpected turns in life that you may come to face.

"What we earn we learn to appreciate,

what we are given the value tends to depreciate."

=Tre Nitty Gritty=

We have to be thankful for history, whether it be the good or the bad experiences that have taken place in the shaping of the world that we live in today. Even when we are in a situation with minimal resources, we have to be able to use our minds as tools to build and create great things that will benefit our lives and the lives of others. Historians have paved many roads for us by creating various inventions.

Things like modern day shelter, electricity, appliances, transportation, means of communication from the postal service to the telephone and these days in time the ultimate gorilla of communication... The internet. These are all things that were created as a result of someone thinking and living rich.

I SPEAK FROM EXPERIENCE, KNOWLEDGE, WISDOM AND UNDERSTANDING.

I'VE EXPERIENCED OR LEARNED FROM OTHER PEOPLES EXPERIENCES AND GAINED KNOWLEDGE.

WITH THAT... I HAVE BECOME FAMILIAR.

MY EXPERIENCE AND KNOWLEDGE TOGETHER GIVES ME THE POWER OF APPLYING WISDOM.

THE INTELLIGENCE AND THE ABILITY TO UNDERSTAND IS THE MASTERY OF UNDERSTANDING.

Understand that there is a need to count your blessings and a need to be thankful for everything under the sun including the dirt for they all serve their own individual purpose as being a part of God's original plan and creation. Be thankful, give thanks and show appreciation.

TOOL # 4

GET ACTIVE / STAY ACTIVE

"ACTIVATE YOUR ACTIVENESS AND STAY ACTIVE IN YOUR ACTIVITIES"

=Tre Nitty Gritty=

Some people will bolt out of the starting blocks full of energy. Half way through the race they may stumble upon a few unexpected hurdles and allow them to interrupt their energetic pattern. As a rich thinker you should use those same unexpected hurdles in life as motivation. Allow them to spike your adrenaline through the roof.

Pick up your pace, lift your head, jump and clear them with ease without losing your stride. Never allow your mind to lose sight of what's beyond the finish line. "THE END GOAL". Either you get active and stay active or you will find yourself in stagnation.

Lacking drive, ambition, motivation and determination the odds of accomplishing the simplest of tasks are slim to none. Set goals and come up with a plan to accomplish them. A plan without action is useless and without goals you are just treadmilling through life with no known destination.

It all starts with your thoughts... That's why exercising your brain is extremely important. The mind has to Get Active / Stay Active as with any other muscle in your body. You must feed it with healthy information, store it and keep it safe.

Protect it by blocking out and rejecting anything negative that will reduce the value of the riches that lie within. Think of your brain as a vault filled with your most prized possessions that are too sacred to place a monetary value upon. =THOUGHT= is a spark to your brain that sends waves to initiate action. Depending on the amount of voltage passing through that spark will determine your response.

In order to Get Active / Stay Active you will have to be fully energized physically and mentally. Get outside, allow the elements of nature to soothe your mind, body and soul. We all need the sun to shine upon us and the fresh air to breeze through us.

Our bodies become accustomed to routine... Do not allow your body to get too familiar with laziness, boredom or stagnation. Your thoughts will influence your mind and your mind will influence your body so Get Active / Stay Active, Think Rich / Live Rich and reap the benefits of living wealthy as the   RICH YOU.

BECOME AN ACTIVE INFLUENCE / REMAIN AN ACTIVE INFLUENCE

INFLUENCE OTHERS TO GET ACTIVE / STAY ACTIVE

The power of influence is immeasurable so be mindful of your actions. You never know who may be paying attention to you and all that you do. You could be a negative influence or a positive influence. Think Rich / Live Rich so that every thought and action will only deliver a clear depiction of what it is to operate in your higher self as the ACTIVE RICH YOU.

TOOL # 5

REPROGRAM YOURSELF

Reprogramming yourself begins with a process of evaluation, unlearning, seeking beneficial information and proper Self-Re-Education. Evaluating the things that we have been taught throughout our lives and separating the valuable from the invaluable.

Growing up we are all subject to the instillation of the beliefs of others whether it be our parents, other family members, friends or school teachers. Religion is the most common, traditional belief of others that we become subject to by default. If the household that you are raised in are followers of a particular religion, the odds of you becoming a follower of that same religion is usually organic.

We are taught that simply questioning religion is a sin and is frowned upon by God resulting in some sort of forsakenness from the Almighty creator, when religion is something that needs to be studied in its entirety in the search of COMPLETE UNDERSTANDING before a commitment or a covenant is made.

HOW COULD ONE HAVE 100% FAITH IN SOMETHING THAT THEY DO NOT 100% UNDERSTAND? =Tre Nitty Gritty=

Until we take control of our own thoughts, exercise our choice and decision-making abilities, it is our faith to lie in the faith of others, believing what they believe based on the belief systems of their influencers. We are all born with the opportunity of choice and the power to make our own decisions. So why are we naturally followers when it comes to certain things?

There is a lot of Merit in the theory of the blind leading the blind. The world today is filled with a lot of blind followers. Sure enough, we all need guidance but if and when you CHOOSE to follow, open your eyes, pay attention to where you are going and know who you are allowing to lead you. There comes a time in life where we will all have to begin thinking for ourselves.

UNTIL WE BEGIN THINKING FOR OURSELVES

WE ARE ALLOWING OTHERS TO DO OUR THINKING FOR US.

=Tre Nitty Gritty=

We all have been exposed to some sort of negative influence in our lives in one way or the other.   What it comes down to is how much of an impact did we ALLOW it to have on us. For some the effect was much more severe than others.

Regardless of the degree

There is a must for the un-learning of all negative thinking and behaviors in order to reprogram your brain to Think Rich so that you can Live Rich.

There is always room for improvement... You should never think or feel that you have reached your peak, as you should never think that you know it all and that there is no need to continue to seek new information for that will only stunt your process of growth. The brain is similar to a computer... It is an open opportunity center that is always available for updates, upgrades and expansion.

I was told that you have two eyes, two ears and only one mouth for three reasons.

1. PAY CLOSE ATTENTION WITH YOUR EYES.

2. LISTEN ATTENTIVELY WITH YOUR EARS.

3. THINK BEFORE YOU SPEAK FOR THE POWER OF THE TONGUE IS IMMEASURABLE.

In order to reprogram yourself you will first have to re-evaluate yourself. Seek information, become aware that there is a need to unlearn all of the negative thoughts and teachings, misguiding and misleading information that we may have received throughout our lives. Feed your brain with valuable information from reliable sources and understand that nothing makes more sense than common sense.

We tend to make things more complicated than they actually are when in all actuality if we were to dumb down our expectations, understand that timing plays a major role in all that we do, we will come to comprehend that there is a necessity for us to take control over our existence.

We have been programmed all of our lives to the liking of someone else's network besides our very own. It is time that we begin to build our own networks and begin working those networks on a quest to reprogram ourselves, steering away from the direction of where we have been being driven without our best interest in mind. We allow ourselves to become programmed whether we pay attention to it or not. As a Rich Thinker you should strive to control your intake so that your program will be made up ONLY of your very own creation.

TOOL #6

TROUBLESHOOTING

What bad habits do you have?

How do they affect you?

Do you abuse alcohol and or tobacco products?

Drugs?

Do you have a hard time finding words to replace foul language?

Do you drown yourself in negative thoughts?

Are you okay with settling for less or expecting nothing from yourself?

Do you set goals but give up before you even get started towards them?

Do you surround yourself with people who release nothing but negative energy into the universe?

THESE ARE NOT WAYS TO RECEIVE RICH RESULTS.

Making poor choices is all a part of life... You have to take it upon yourself to do your own **TROUBLESHOOTING.** Identifying your truth and correcting your decision making for it is a necessity in order for you to have the ability to Think Rich / Live Rich.

It takes YOU to take NOTICE...

Then take ACTION

=Tre Nitty Gritty=

The circle that you choose to surround yourself with can do 1 of 3 things.

1. Lift you up and propel you forward.
2. Drag you down and hold you back.
3. Keep you stuck in place going nowhere.

Remove yourself from any situation that has the potential of hindering the expansion of your mind or the growth of your existence. If anything has a negative effect on you or in your life you have to trim away the excess non-beneficial elements or else it will taint and tarnish you.

TRUTH BE TOLD... THERE IS A DIFFERENCE BETWEEN "TRUTH" AND "BELIEF"

=Tre Nitty Gritty=

=Truth= is "fact" ... Something of quality or in the state of being true.

=Belief = is a form of "Opinion" The acceptance of being, trust or confidence in being truthful.

You have to be truthful with yourself about the trouble areas in your life that are in need of maintenance. You may "Believe" that you do not have any area that is in need of an adjustment but the "Truth" may state otherwise.

You can't LIE to or FOOL anyone but YOURSELF

So, be TRUTHFUL with YOURSELF and FACE YOUR TRUTH... =Tre Nitty Gritty=

TOOL # 7

POWER THINKING

In order to be a POWER THINKER, your thinking has to be SHARP and EFFECTIVE.

You cannot allow outside influences to distract you from your thoughts.

AS A RICH THINKER YOUR THOUGHTS

ARE YOUR PERSONAL GOLDMINE

Imagination holds more value than knowledge... For, knowledge is limited but imagination has no boundaries. You have to tap into your powers of creativity and get creative with the riches of the oil that exists beneath your earth's surface. Don't just think... THINK BIG! Don't just make moves, Make POWER MOVES and move as a POWER THINKER.

Some say that it doesn't cost you anything to pay attention but I would have to disagree with that statement. Anything that you are giving your undivided attention to is costing you time... And time is precious.

PAY ATTENTION

TO WHAT YOU ARE PAYING ATTENTION TO

BECAUSE YOU ARE PAYING WITH TIME.

=Tre Nitty Gritty=

Time is something that doesn't stop, pause or rewind and once you lose it you cannot get it back. Make the best use of your time and do not waste it by paying attention to frivolous things or engaging in frivolous conversations. Power thinking is thinking things all the way through to the end... There is a famous saying that you should always **"BEGIN WITH THE END IN MIND"**.

You have to have a vivid imagination and visualize things as if they are directly in front of you. Consider all the risk factors in all that you do for losing is all a part of winning. In other words, you should expect to lose at some point in time on your journey towards becoming successful.

NO STRUGGLE / NO PROGRESS

NO PAIN / NO GAIN

THE ONLY ONES WHO HAVE NEVER FAILED

ARE THOSE WHO HAVE NEVER TRIED

You have to be a risk taker but be aware of the risk that you take. Always calculate the odds and weigh your options. Just as you think your way into a situation, you have to be a power thinker and be able to think you way out of that same situation by implementing an exit strategy into your planning from the very beginning as with buildings that are equipped with fire escape routes and or cellars that are built to protect those from tornadoes or some other natural disaster that may occur at some point in time.

Your thoughts hold a tremendous amount of power.

Thoughts build empires.

Thoughts bring things into existence.

Thoughts change lives. Once you become a MASTER OF YOUR THOUGHTS...

You will elevate to the level of a POWER THINKER, with that reaching the level of a MASTERMIND

TOOL # 8

COMMUNICATION

Being that communication rules the nation, learning communication skills should be high on your list of priorities. There are many different forms of communication from traditional speaking to sign language, body language, reading and writing. Every species on earth has their own way of communicating. Babies cry, Dogs bark, birds chirp, lions roar, wolves howl, snakes hiss. Regardless of nature, we are all living beings with the need to be able to communicate. In different areas of the world, there are different dominant languages that are translatable with one another providing us with the ability to communicate on a global level.

As a Rich Thinker you have to use communication as a building tool. Lacking the ability to communicate can cause destruction before construction of a valuable relationship. One small disagreement can turn into a complicated life ling situation of being at odds with someone who we could have possibly communicated in a different manner with that may have resulted in a different outcome. A fruitful conversation can very easily turn into a useless debate. Learn to recognize rotten fruit before indulging. It could prove to be the difference between life and death, profit or loss, financial gain or financial despair. Being able to communicate "EFFECTIVELY" can be the tool to opening doors that you never knew existed. It could land you on a level of heights well beyond your imagination. If you happen to communicate yourself into a room of CEO/Business people you would then have to have the ability to speak and also understand their language.

It's not always "WHAT" you say, but more so "HOW" you say it and it's not always "WHAT" you hear but more so "HOW" you "RECEIVE" it. Once you are able to deliver and receive information, respond effectively and accordingly this is a true sign of having great communication skills.

To some this is a natural gift that can be utilized with ease. For others, it takes studying and practice to perfect but the value of it is something more than worth the pursuit to obtain.

COMMUNICATION

&

EFFECTIVE CONVERSATION

CAN LEAD YOU TO A DESTINATION

BEYOND YOUR WILDEST DREAMS

SO, COMMUNICATE & ELEVATE.

There is nothing wrong with being antisocial at times but some situations call for direct contact and communication in order for you to reach the next level of life. We have the ability to communicate our way to success. All we have to do is realize how much of an effect we have when communicating and maximize our potential. The power that the Tongue possesses is something that scientists have yet come to find out.

TOOL # 9

PATIENCE

When they say patience is a virtue that means that it is a good quality trait to have. It is a form of effective inherent power. A great characteristic attribute. We have a patience for things to come into fruition in life. It takes seasons for things to produce, that is just one of the laws of nature.

There is a time for planting, a time for nurturing, a time for growth and a time to reap benefits.   There is a combination of things that go into the process of production. If you do not follow the procedure or attempt to skip some of the simplest of steps the results you will receive will in-turn mirror your impatience, it will be clearly visible and noticeable.

Times when you find yourself in a rush, thinking or saying "I can't wait" or "I can't do". Slow down, stop, curve your thoughts and reword your vocabulary. Tell yourself "I can wait" or "I can do" and reap the benefits of utilizing =transformational vocabulary=

Relax and allow this rebuttal to resonate as you shift your thoughts from poor to rich thinking you will receive the glory and the power of having patience. Any time that you rush through anything, you are taking a chance at missing out on something, often possibly a major attribute into whatever the endeavor may be that you are in the process of pursuing.

Being in a rush to get through with anything isn't always the answer. Imagine speed reading through a book in preparation for a final exam.

You are liable to miss out on some vital information that you would have more than likely recognized if you were to read it slowly word for word, study it and re-read it. Even when time isn't on your side, it is better to make the best use of the time that you do have being that you don't have any time to make or fix any mistakes. Master the art of having patience... Do not panic at the hands of time, instead make time work in your favor. You have to have perseverance and the ability to endure the wait, the tolerance to control your anxiety, the restraint to resist temptation and overpower your thoughts of the quick and easy let's get it over with mentality.

The wait,

The buildup

The anticipation of the high point

Only intensifies the grand finale.

=Tre Nitty Gritty=

Take your time and enjoy your meal instead of devouring it greedily. Don't be a gluten in life. Cherishing the precious moments of time for immediate gratification can overpower our sense of realistic reasonableness. These are the times when our process of thought and patience has to be at its richest.

TOOL # 10

OBSERVANCE

Everything on earth has and serves its own purpose. It is all a matter of how observant we are and how deep we look into things with our imperial eye. For instance... A tree is a living and breathing element of the earth and serves multiple purposes to our environment.

A tree is a major contributing factor to the air that we breathe. It proves to be a home and shelter to some animals and insects. It also stands to be a natural healthy food source provider for us all as a whole. Its wood is known to be used in many different forms in the world today. It is known to be used to create paper, building matter. You have to identify all of your contributing factors. Ask yourself, honestly...

What are my capabilities?

What can I do to better myself and in-turn assist with the improvement of others?

How can I assist with the growth of the universe?

What is my purpose on this earth?

How can I make a difference?

STEP OUTSIDE YOURSELF

&

TAKE A LOOK AT YOURSELF

Through self-observation you will accomplish the task of seeing yourself outside of yourself. Step outside of your body and take a look in the mirror. Observe yourself in full from head to toe, inside out. Only you can truly accomplish the goal of taking a look at the real you being that you are the only person who can truly know who you really are. Others only know what they observe of the outer you when the inner-you is the only REAL you.

A lot of us have walls built up preventing anyone from getting to know the true us. These walls a lot of times are built up from past experiences and events that have taken place in our lives. Most believe that this is the easiest way to avoid reliving or experiencing these events all over again. Though the truth is that the observance of these events, feelings and emotions has more power than the avoidance… So, observe them and master them.

Face them and figure out how to make them serve as =tools= for you to face your past and build your future. These are all simple lessons of life and in life experience is the best teacher of them all. You can put up a front and portray to be someone who you are not providing a false image for the observance of others misleading their judgment of your character. At some point in time everything done in the dark will come to the light.

Get to know your true TALENTS for they could prove to make a drastic difference in your life and the lives of others. Get to know your FLAWS... The more you know about them the less likely you are to make a costly mistake. This is the benefit of having self-awareness and observing yourself in complete form.

Practice becoming self-observant on a daily basis. Identifying who you are will open your eyes to the abilities that you possess. Paying attention and having a clear observation of the people, places and things around you at all times is one of the most valuable rules of survival.

You can unknowingly place yourself around someone or somewhere and become subject to a situation that has nothing to do with you whatsoever. If you are able to take notice of this there is a chance that you may be able to remove yourself from that situation before being removed by an unforeseen force.

If you fail to be observant it could cost you dearly. There are times when you may feel a bad vibe about a person or being in a certain place. In times like these you need to listen to and follow your gut feeling. Usually, it is the right thing to do because even if you aren't right, you could be wrong and as the saying goes... It is better to be safe than to be sorry.

BECOME A PERIPHERAL VISIONIST

AND MASTER THE ART OF SEEING ALL THINGS

EVEN WHEN THEY ARE NOT

IN YOUR DIRECT LINE OF SIGHT

=Tre Nitty Gritty=

Keep your head on a swivel even when looking straight ahead. Utilize your sense to perceive and even without physically touching. Use your intuitive awareness, intelligence, perception and quick wideness then continue to move about with observance.

BOSS UP

B.Y.O.B.

"BECOME YOUR OWN BOSS" BUILD YOUR OWN BUSINESS"

AND BECOME YOUR OWN BRAND

=Tre Nitty Gritty=

There are two types of people in this world. You have Bosses and you have Workers... Employers and Employees. As the laws that govern human nature would have it every worker is not fit to be a boss and every boss is not fit to be a worker. As a Rich Thinker, take the time to analyze yourself. Once you honestly come to realistic terms of where you stand "BOSS UP" and become the CEO of your life.

Regardless if you are a BOSS or a WORKER you do not want to become a slave for money. You have to make money become your slave and make it work for you. In order to become successful with mastering money it is going to take strict discipline and financial literacy.

Most people spend money long before they even have it in their possession. Whether they are working to earn a week-to-week paycheck from an average 9 to 5 job or playing the lottery and hoping one day to strike it rich.

I always hear conversations where people will say "If I had a million dollars" I would buy this and I would purchase that. "I'd retire and never have to work again but the truth is as it stands. If you have exactly 1 million dollars in your possession, the moment that you spend one penny you are no longer a millionaire. Also, if you are not working or putting your money to work for you the odds of you colliding head-to-head with financial failure are much more likely.

This is why Thinking Rich and Living Rich goes hand in hand. You cannot GET RICH if you are not THINKING RICH and if you are not THINKING RICH, you cannot LIVE RICH. You have to know that you have the ability to make something out of nothing. You have to think of ways to take what you have and build an enterprise then turn that enterprise into an empire.

Get educated on ways to incorporate, ways to turn your company into a brand then expand your brand into a franchise. Think of ways to save money, ways to make money, make a profit and capitalize on the return on your investments. Learn how to get rich off of other people's money without investing a dime, only your time. Understand the importance of having a strong and effective team... Then BUILD ONE.

KEEP IN MIND THAT A BUILDING

IS ONLY AS STRONG AS ITS FOUNDATION

SO, MAKE SURE THAT YOUR FOUNDATION

IS SOLID AND FIRM

Learn how to maneuver through life as a corporate body. Stand on the shoulders of corporate giants and study their moves. Learn what "NOT" to do and what "TO" do then "DO IT"! You will only get as rich as your ideas though your ideas can bring you an unexpected amount of wealthiness.

BEING YOUR OWN BOSS

YOU ARE RESPONSIBLE FOR YOUR OWN

SUCCESS OR FAILURE

Just as the Boss of a business is responsible for their company's success or failure. Many people tend to place the blame of failed attempts onto the shoulders of others but love to take claim and receive all the glory for their successful endeavors.

A true Boss knows and understands that any failed plan begins and ends with them and is willing to take full responsibility for either or. You cannot have success without failure so accept where you fail then strive to succeed.

If you are a worker, set your goals high and be the best worker for the job. Be in the best condition for the position. If the job entails physical work make sure that you are physically fit. Hard labor can be hard on the body so work hard and work out even harder.

If your job requires a lot of mental effort, then you need to train your brain for the task at hand. Study, study, study... Strengthen your brain so that it functions to its highest potential. Learn the ins and outs of your job's details. Work diligently at work and outside of work to always remain ahead of the curve.

This is called "BOSSING YOURSELF AROUND"

Get the best job that you can land assuring that it is worth the time that you are investing. If you are going to spend 8 to 12 or more hours a day at a workplace, I would imagine that you would want to make as much money as possible when doing so.

Know that every day that you are working you are paving the road to your future. Work hard, save money, find something to invest into and no matter what you do make sure that you are living within your means... Not outside of them.

Keep your income high and your bills, necessities, responsibilities and liabilities as low as possible. Instead of just renting a home, rent to OWN a home or if possible, purchase one. Instead of leasing or financing a vehicle, buy a vehicle that fits into your budget instead of trying to fit instead of trying to fit into what is popular.

Continue to save money and upgrade once the opportunity presents itself, just remember... The main objective is ownership. Interest rates are never in your best interest... "UNLESS" of course you are "THE DEALER". =Tre Nitty Gritty=

If ever the day comes that you decide being a worker isn't working for you and you develop a thirst for entrepreneurship... "BOSS UP "and make the transition. As long as you have achieved your high school diploma or General Equivalency Diploma / G.E.D. You have the option of furthering your education onto the college level. If you not have either one, obtain either or, If for no other reason... Do it for yourself. There are community colleges in your area that you can attend. Walk in and apply in person or call and set up an appointment with administration over the phone. Fact of the matter is there is a need to continue to seek information for the more you know the more you grow.

If more convenient, there are a plethora of online colleges that you can apply to and if eligible, receive financial aid and student loan / grant benefits even without living in the same city or state that the school is located. Find a course / major that holds your interest, for the more interested in something you are the higher the possibility you have at excelling in that particular field.

Me, personally... If I am going to spend valuable time going to college, I am going to make sure that the payoff will be monumental. Not just for bragging rights of a title or certain level of a college degree. How will this benefit you in your personal life? Will you still have to apply and search for a job once you finish with your schooling? Will it be worth the cost that you are paying financially or the debt that you will have acquired by the time you are finished?

Make sure that the skills that you pursue are able to produce profits, then put your =tools= to work. Dedicate yourself to mastering your craft. If you have a hobby, turn your hobby to a business. There is nothing greater than to be getting paid for something that you love to do.

TOOL # 12

AVOID BLOOD SUCKERS

&

DREAM KILLERS

Stay away from blood suckers & dream killers. People with no goals, no ambition and negative mind states will attempt to convince you into their way of thinking and their way of living. They will suck the life out of your positive energy and kill your dreams. These types of people will hold you back in life simply to have someone to accompany them with doing absolutely nothing at all.

They live to talk about others behind their backs, complain about how boring life is and block your vision any time that you have something positive on the horizon. They will destroy your plans before you even put your plans together, not even giving you a chance to put your plans into action. Most of these blood suckers and dream killers can't see past their own misery.

They are not bosses nor are they workers... They are negative energy at its highest capacity. They'd rather complain and come up with a thousand excuses of why they can't get a job or how nobody will hire them when there are thousands of job opportunities available to them. Not to mention the one that you have the most control over and that is =Bossing up=. Building your own business and becoming your own brand.

They have thousands of excuses as to why the world will not allow them or you to be successful at being the owner of any business. This is why it is a must that you stay as far away from them as possible.

THEY ARE INFECTED

AND THE DISEASE THAT THEY CARRY

IS TRANSFERABLE BY SIMPLY

SHARING THE SAME AIR THAT THEY BREATHE.

=Tre Nitty Gritty=

Their negative vibes are contagious... Keep your distance or you will be subject to being exposed to their poisonous ways killing your drive and determination, ultimately causing you to become a blood sucker and a dream killer such as they are.

BEWARE OF THE COMPANY YOU KEEP

FOR BLOOD SUCKERS AND DREAM KILLERS

WILL DRAIN YOU

UNTIL YOU BECOME WEAK

=Tre Nitty Gritty=

TOOL # 13

STAY IN YOUR OWN LANE

Staying in your own lane is like driving solo on an open road with little to no traffic. You are in complete control of your commute. Even during rush hour when traffic is congested and backed up bumper to bumper. As long as you stay alert and aware of your surroundings, what's going on in the lanes along the sides of you are none of your concern.

Until you are met with the threat of immediate danger veering into your path, continue to proceed with caution and stay in your own lane. Just because something works for someone else doesn't mean that you should set aside what you do to jump onto their band wagon.

Become a master of YOUR gifts...

Sharpen YOUR tools,

exercise YOUR talents,

stick to YOUR script,

give it YOUR all.

Do not allow someone to talk you into gambling if gambling isn't your cup of tea. If you have that bad gut feeling once again... Listen to it. It could possibly be saving you from losing a lot of money or picking up a nasty habit that has addiction written all over it.

TOOL # 14

GROWTH

"Growing up" is all a part of "Growing apart"

from certain

PEOPLE, PLACES, THINGS, THOUGHTS, GOALS, FEELINGS AND EMOTIONS.

=Tre Nitty Gritty=

From the moment that we are conceived we begin to grow. There comes a time when as a fetus that we outgrow out mother's womb, begin to kick and fight causing her to go into labor, delivering us from the only world we know at the time, introducing us to an entirely new world filled with unlimited opportunities. We go from crying when in need of being fed or having our diapers changed to feeding ourselves and being potty trained. We go from lying around to crawling, we begin standing, then walking, talking, running, reading, writing, riding bikes, exploring and experiencing life growing up.

Growing is a natural progression of nature... Through a combination of components all things come into existence. We are born, we live, then we die. The difference between wildlife nature and human nature is the levels of work that the human being is capable of accomplishing. Sure enough, animals and insects have the power to reproduce, feed themselves and acquire a habitat for shelter but humans can excel well beyond the heights and limitations that animals and insects are subject to.

NEGATIVE CIRCLES GET SMALLER

AS THE MIND EXPANDS OF A RICH THINKER

MAKING ROOM FOR THE GROWTH

AND DEVELOPMENT OF NEW THINGS

TO COME INTO FRUITION

=Tre Nitty Gritty=

A part of growing up is growing apart from certain people whom we may have been blessed to experience a period of our growth process with. Simply knowing someone as far back as you can remember doesn't necessarily mean that you will grow in sync and head into the same directions in life. If you do not take notice and take action when it is time to sever ties and move into your own direction there is a force of gravitation that will pull you in a direction of its own.

You can attend the same elementary school with someone and by the time the two of you reach middle or high school be on two completely different paths in life. Some people jump heavy into sports or dive deep into education. Others may venture off into exploring a world of drugs and criminal activity. At this point in life is what we call the fork in the road. The time to make a decision and choose the path of your desire.

What happens here depends heavily on our influences... and influencers... Some are more fortunate than others to have a caring and concerned support system. That system has the power to influence them and provide them with a vision of a bright future and drive them towards pursuing positive goals.

Others who are less fortunate are subject to poverty and negative influence, influencing them in ways that their behavior could possibly worsen their condition of living contrary to bettering their situation. Growing apart from someone is in no way looking down upon or feeling and thinking like you are better than the next person. It is not about degrading or belittling other human beings.

It is simply a matter of recognizing your path, staying on it and away from anyone who isn't heading in the same direction.... You cannot mix with people who aren't into what you are into. Similar to water and oil... You can attempt to put the two of them together but they will be forever separated for they do not mix.

In the process of growth, it is imperative to change your thoughts and the process of your thinking. If you do not outgrow your old ways you will find yourself stuck in them.

AT SOME POINT IN TIME

THINGS GET OLD

AND THER COMES A TIME FOR A CHANGE

=Tre Nitty Gritty=

Believe it or not, there are many people who have never ventured outside of their very own neighborhoods, cities, states etc. They have never stepped outside of their comfort zone and have not even attempted to explore the world to at least see what it has to offer. They are content with where they are and what they have.

Seeing and experiencing new things is the only way to expand your horizon. If you have no knowledge of something existing you are oblivious to it. Until you step out and experience the world it will not become a part of your reality. Similar to never leaving the nest of your family's residence and standing up on your own two feet, transitioning from a dependent to an independent adult.

A lot of people have a fear of the "UNKNOWN". They fear being uncomfortable, they fear failure, they fear new places, they fear trying new things, they fear growth, they fear life and they fear death. Sometimes you have to take a step out onto the ledge and take a chance. Get the feel of trying and experiencing new things.

Going to new places, meeting new people, becoming familiar with traveling. Stepping outside of your comfort zone can open your eyes to new opportunities that you never would have known existed had you stayed confined within your box.

Once you become an active traveler you will begin to notice others who are stuck in the same place doing the same things. No matter how long you are away, upon your return you will become more aware of the stagnant being stagnant.

A lot of times this means that your growth has begun to sprout. You have to come to the realization that the things that once appeared to be large in your eyes are now becoming smaller in your new broadened vision. The things that used to impress you no longer impress you. The things that once satisfied you no longer give you satisfaction.

You'll begin to develop a thirst and an appetite for more. Your desire will push you to demand what you deserve. Your curiosity will influence you to seek and you will begin to push yourself towards achieving what you are craving. There will be nothing strong enough to stand in your way once you conquer your own self-disablement. Relationships will change, your environment will shift, your thinking will elevate, your progress will amplify and the results of your actions will pay off tremendously.

Do not stop growing and do not place limitations upon yourself. As you expand, develop a new network by making new connections. Set long term goals and take the necessary steps to reach them. Laying one brick today will build tomorrow's empire.

TOOL # 15

PREPARATION

In any task... Training and preparation is a high priority. Skipping the process of prepping could cost you. From the very beginning you have to prepare your plot and prepare your plan for if you are not prepared you are unprepared. The purpose of a blueprint is the planning and preparation of a particular design.

A print of detailed plans consisting of precise angels, measurements, numbers and calculations that will be necessary for it to be assembled. In day-to-day life when we wake up, we have to prepare ourselves for the day's activities. We have to dress accordingly for whatever the occasion may be.

If your agenda is aligned with doing yard work, I would assume that you wouldn't dress yourself in the best attire from your closet. "Vise, versa" ... If you are preparing yourself for a job interview or a business meeting that requires cleanliness, I'm sure you wouldn't show up in grass stains.

There is a reason why when someone signs up to join the military, they are first to participate in an intense bootcamp training. It is for the preparation of what "POSSIBLY" lies ahead. Whether or not they end up on the frontlines of a battlefield they have to first be prepared for combat. Though this day may or may not present itself, the possibility alone calls for immediate preparation.

They cannot be relied upon in the field without the knowledge, experience and the confidence that it takes to be a dependable soldier with the ability to endure pressure and perform under intense circumstances. You have to think ahead, prepare and expect the unexpected.

Throughout life we are all taught the process of preparation. Whether we take notice of how important it is or not all depends on the sight and scope of our own vision. At home we prepare for the day, at school we prepare for tests, during the orientation of a job we are being prepared for our position.

In college we are prepping for the field of work that we will be entering upon our graduation. Taking a test to receive our driver's license is preparing us for the road and being able to lawfully operate a motor vehicle. Education is preparing... Teaching, instruction and development. Planting rich seeds in order to receive rich benefits.

By providing ourselves with the tools of preparation we are equipping ourselves with the ability to arm others with the tools to become their rich selves.

LAYING THE GROUNDWORK IS THE FOUNDATION

TENDING TO THE LAND BECOMES THE

RESPONSABILITY

=Tre Nitty Gritty=

=TOOL= # 16

LIVE THE DREAM

THE DIFFERENCE BETWEEN HAVING A DREAM

AND LIVING THE DREAM

IS TAKING ACTION.

Most of us tend to view our dreams as a vision. Something that is "APART" from us, far away in the distance that we must travel down long winding roads to achieve. Something that is "OUTSIDE" of our reach that we have to work towards in order to feel the satisfaction of its presence in our lives.

OUR DREAMS ARE NOT

APART

"FROM US"

THEY ARE

A PART

"OF US"

Our dreams give us drive and motivation to make them become a part of our reality but they reality is that they are already amongst us the moment that we produce the thought... We just have to live the dream. Living the dream is a mind state turned into an action. Knowing that who you want to be you already are, you simply have to begin to operate in that order.

Dreams don't just come true;

they are made true by the dreamer.

Thinking Rich is the dream itself...

Living rich is the act of

=Living the Dream=.

Dreams and nightmares are one in the same to a certain extent. If you have nightmares of failing and losing everything that you have worked hard to achieve... Those same nightmares can be used as the fuel to the fire that pushes you towards successful heights that you never knew existed.

As long as you direct the energy that they give you into the right direction and apply it properly you will come to realize that you are in complete control over whether or not you are dreaming or living the dream. The more vivid the dream the more you will believe in it. Your conscious and unconscious minds will begin to work in alignment with one another bringing your dreams to a reality.

LIVE YOUR DREAMS

DON'T LIVE IN REGRET

=Tre Nitty Gritty=

Success lies in the power of your THINKING and the DRIVE behind your determination. Your thoughts have power and influence, as do your dreams. How much power and influence do your thoughts have over your actions? How much do they motivate you?

You have to understand that your dreams are not something that belongs to the future. They belong to you and wherever you choose to place them. You have to place your dreams in the now... Live in the moment. You cannot get rich in the future and you cannot get rich in the past. You can only get rich and live rich in the present.

TOMORROW ISN'T PROMISED

AND YESTERDAY WILL NEVER RETURN

THEREFORE, GO FOR WHAT YOU KNOW

RIGHT HERE / RIGHT NOW

=Tre Nitty Gritty=

You have to take the necessary steps to get to where you are heading. Thoughts and dreams come to you

but success doesn't. You will have to meet it halfway. Yet, this does not mean that you will only have to put in half of the effort. Give it your all and all shall come together organically.

Your dreams are visions of your thoughts...

Think Rich, Dream Rich and

=Live Your Dreams=...

Surround yourself with people who inspire one another. It is important to have positive energy to latch onto in order to keep you fully charged. People, places and things can assist you with the mission of living your dreams. You will only grow as big as your imagination and your network so get busy imagining and networking. Building relationships and bridges that will accelerate your growth and get you where you are striving to be in life.

Bounce around ideas, stay open for suggestions, give positive feedback, and accept constructive criticism. Put into practice what you learn and =use your tools=. If you do not use what you know then what you know is useless.

Do not allow the time that you have spent studying, researching and schooling all go to waste. Make the best use of your efforts, your assets, your skills / talents, gifts and abilities. This is called capitalizing off of effective thinking by taking effective action.

DREAM CHASERS CHASE AFTER DREAMS WHILE DREAM CATCHERS CATCH DREAMS AND LIVE THEM.

=Tre Nitty Gritty=

Utilize your dreams for everything that they are worth. Your dreams can influence the dreams of others. Your dreams could be worth millions better yet BILLIONS!... Your dreams could change your life and the lives of others.

When you have a passion for something that means that you have a strong mental connection to a certain object, craving, thirst, desire or hunger for it. That force will navigate you through the terrain and get you through the trials and tribulations that will present themselves as you begin living your dreams.

If you can imagine it, you can have it...

If you can think it, you can achieve it.

Don't just dream of being a star... Activate your star power and BE a star.

Don't just dream of being a boss... MOVE LIKE A BOSS...

Your actions will begin to shape your life into what you have envisioned that was once just a dream, all because you began =LIVING THE DREAM=.

TOOL # 17

NO DAYS OFF

Doing NOTHING, will get you NOTHING... So do not let a day go past without doing "SOMETHING". There is no such thing as taking a day off. If you are not doing one thing you could be doing another. At times you may slow up your pace and take a break to catch your breath but never stop moving completely.

The mind is always at work though there comes a time and a need for rest to recharge in order for the brain to function to its full potential. Get a few hours of sleep or take a power nap but avoid taking a full 24 hours off...

24 hours is too long to go without getting "SOMETHING" done. Once you become accustomed to taking care of business, experiencing growth and expansion... Being idle will begin to feel foreign to you. Your inner-self will not allow you to sit around and do absolutely "NOTHING".

The main ones that you hear complain about needing a day off are usually workers... Even then, once they receive their paycheck they usually regret missing a day of work. Bosses are usually busy trying to find more work for their workers and ways to capitalize off of their workers capabilities.

Days off for a boss, in their eyes, is a loss... They are always looking for more ways to continue operations with as minimal shut down as possible. Why do you think they offer more pay for overtime hours and that there is such an incentive as holiday pay?

A worker works to earn paid vacation time, while a Boss takes vacations that usually turn out to be business meetings. A Boss is at work, even when he isn't at work. Get out and get it while the rest of the world sleeps. By the time they wake they will be spending their time attempting to catch up. You will be so far ahead of the race, that as long as you maintain a steady pace you will easily run laps around them and seize the victory.

When you don't feel like doing anything at all and find yourself sitting around being lazy... You have to revert back to having =Rich Self Talk= and motivate yourself to =Get Active / Stay Active=. Getting to work when you don't feel like working is the most effective way of interrupting the pattern of being lazy. By breaking the pattern, you will begin to steer away from the habit of "Not Doing". You will also begin to realize that once you get started, the feeling of laziness will disappear and you will accomplish some of your greatest work. Be MOTIVATED by the UNMOTIVATED. Strive to achieve the results that the lazy are too lazy to obtain.

Never start something without finishing it... No matter how long it takes, the determined will never give up. Continue your mission and see it all the way through to the end. Taking days off can take away your drive and hinder your motivation. You will find yourself in pursuit of more and more days off. Eventually this will become a pattern and end up costing you more than you will gain from it.

You will lose more than you will benefit by simply operating in the wrong are of satisfaction. You could lose your job, lose your vehicle, or lose your home all because you lost your spark. So, instead of taking the day off... Make your day pay off.

TOOL # 18

EVERY DOLLAR COUNTS

Regardless of how you look at it, every penny, nickel, dime and quarter add up to dollars and every dollar counts. Whether you are doing addition, subtraction, multiplication or division. Money saved is money earned... Having the ability to hold onto your money is the first step to keeping it. The second step is finding out how, and where to invest it so that it accumulates instead of disintegrating.

In a sense, having money is similar to playing a game of numbers. Once you become a master of the game you will become a master of money instead of being a slave to it. Money has its powers... It can give people a sense of security.it could mean the difference between eating or starving, having a home or being homeless.

Money has the power to stir many of our emotions causing an intense feeling to rush through our bodies. Money is a heartless and emotionless element. It doesn't love anyone, yet the majority of us develop a love for money and or the things that money can do for us when in reality money can't do anything for us. We do things for ourselves WITH money.

We have to come to the realization that we are the money masters...

We are in complete control but at times we tend to lose control for we become emotionally invested and begin attaching money to a number of our emotions.

This is a strong, mental and emotional entanglement that we place ourselves in. A lot of times we do this unbeknownst to our knowledge being that we are moving off of sheer emotion and not logic. Especially when our responsibilities are applying what seems to be tons of pressure upon us. We are drawn towards and driven by our "Love" for material things, the "feeling" of gratification, the" thought" of being worry free, the "Illusion" of being rich and the "idea" of living wealthy.

We relate the "fear" of going without to the "urge" of having more. With that, intensifying our emotions and feelings of failure. In doing this, money can easily become our "RULER" and once money becomes the "RULER" of you... You have given it all of the power that it needs to "RUIN" you. No dollar amount will suffice for your appetite, quench your thirst or fulfill your hunger for more. This is usually when the root of evil is planted and begins to sprout.

IF YOU DO NOT KILL THE MONSTER

WHILE IT IS SMALL

YOU WILL HAVE A FULL GROWN

SAVAGE BEAST ON YOUR HANDS

LATER ON, DOWN THE LINE

Devilish things will begin to cross your mind like lies, deceit and manipulation. Conniving, scheming, trickery and scandalous ways will come to surface at the forefront of your thought process. You will begin to act in ways that are outside of your natural character because you are no longer the master of your emotions.

Your emotions are now being mastered by money and the satisfaction that it delivers to your inner-demons. They whisper, they scream... and they will continue to live as long as you continue to feed and breathe life into them.

Imaginary money can be similar to a magnet... Acting as an unseen force of gravitation pulling us towards something that only exists on the inside of our minds. Some of the things that I have seen people do for this imaginary fortune have been mind-blowing. Some come up with the craziest of ideas or get rich quick schemes even when they are the most immoral and unethical.

They will sacrifice themselves or others by creating life threatening circumstances and situations that will be next to impossible to survive through or difficult to come out unscathed from. The imagination is so strong that it will draw you towards this imaginary money with both of your eyes closed and a blindfold blocking the sight of your common sense.

THE IMAGINATION IS

FUELED BY INFATUATION

=Tre Nitty Gritty=

Money comes in many different forms whether it be the most common form of cash... The promissory note / I-owe-you. Money also comes in the form of paper checks, coins, debit / credit and or crypto currency. In the end, it all reverts back to its original origin of "NUMBERS". Numbers that are for counting. Accounting, keeping track of and monitoring for every penny that is earned to every dollar that is spent because every dollar counts.

As a rich thinker, your thoughts have to be superior over your emotions, for if you do not do the thinking for your emotions they will react without your best interest in mind. If you are emotionally attached to money, the loss of finances can prove to be devastating. Some have gone to the extent of committing suicide after experiencing a financial crisis.

Some have stolen from family members or committed senseless crimes and ended up in jail in the pursuit of lost wages simply because they were emotionally distraught after losing all of the finances that they possessed due to bad decision making and having poor money management skills.

WHEN THE VALUE OF MONEY BECOMES MORE SUPERIOR THAN YOUR PERSONAL VALUES YOUR VALUES ARE VALUELESS

=Tre Nitty Gritty=

=TOOL= # 19

BALANCE

Balance is a very important aspect into Thinking Rich and Living Rich. You have to have the ability to balance yourself and stand as an independent THINKING and independent LIVING individual centering yourself upon your central pivot point maintaining your =BALANCE=.

BALANCE IS A VERY NECESSARY

ATTRIBUTE FOR THE STABILITY

OF THE BODY & THE MIND.

=Tre Nitty Gritty=

Without balance of the body, you cannot stand and without balance of the mind your thought process will be unsteady. Balance is the result of a group effort of four different directions. North, South, East & West. Once these are established it takes balance to maintain stability. Once you gain control, maintain control of your equilibrium being that is your state of physical and mental balance.

This constitutes your state of composure so manage your steadiness and evenness with awareness and intelligence. Every human being has a spiritual makeup of a "Higher-Self" and a "Lower-Self". That is just a part of our natural existence. As humans, we have the ability of choosing in which "SELF" we operate. This goal should consist of operating in ones ``HIGHER-SELF" as often as possible.

It's all in scientific order, similar to the earth's need for balance. The earth needs a certain amount of rain balanced with an appropriate amount of sun in order for the earth to function and operate productively. Too much of one or the other will cause droughts and or death to people, places and things proving that =Balance= Is essential.

In life there are a number of things that we would not be able to either enjoy nor know to appreciate without having the opposing element to balance them out. "For instance," What would sunny days be without rainy days? When it is hot outside for too long a period of time, we find ourselves yearning for rain either to water our grass, plants and produce, trees or simply for a change in climate.

There would be no right without left, no up without down, no high without low, no big without small, no good without bad. There is a time when there is a need for the use of scorching hot water just as there are other times when there is a need for ice cold water. Oftentimes there is a necessity for there to be a =BALANCE= between the two and for the water to be used at a warm or room temperature.

How much would we appreciate happy times without having experience of the sad ones? How could we experience joy or even have knowledge of its existence without at some point experiencing pain? Could there be good without evil? Furthermore, was the thought of God vs the Devil developed to keep us as human beings in =BALANCE=? Whether we want to accept it or not we are all born with an evil gene somewhere within us. There are certain things that may trigger us in an attempt to knock us off =balance=... It is up to us how we react when that situation presents itself.

Would there be angels without demons? Would there be order without disorder? Would there be any balance in the world if people didn't believe that there was a Heaven or Hell that they will be transitioning to in the afterlife and the one that they end up spending eternity at all depends on the things that they do while here on this earth?

THE KEY IS TO INSTRUCT ORDER

CONTROL YOUR BALANCE

OPERATE IN YOUR RIGHT MIND

OVER YOUR WRONG MIND...

YOUR STRONG MIND

OVER YOUR WEAK MIND.

This will bring you =balance=, health, wealth, security, prosperity, confidence, influence, worthiness, love, elevation, success, blessings, healing, knowledge, wisdom, understanding, power, intelligence and independence.

WITHOUT BALANCE, ONE CANNOT STAND...

DEVELOP BALANCE OF YOUR MIND,

BODY AND SOUL THEN, MAINTAIN STABILITY.

=Tre Nitty Gritty=

TOOL # 20

THINK OUTSIDE THE BOX

Thinking outside of the box is an action of a RICH THINKER. A lot of us tend to stay trapped inside of our own minds and cannot see past the enclosure that we have confined ourselves within. Most of the time we form a wall that is too tall for even us ourselves to see over. We lack the drive to climb and the strength to tear it down.

We fear what is on the outside so we become comfortable within the space of our very own creation limiting our possibilities for growth or success. You could be sitting next to someone who could change your life forever in some way, shape or form but if your fears and insecurities deter you from approaching situations in an attempt to open doors you will not be able to develop into a Rich Thinker...

Life is like a maze... There are many roads that take you in circles leading you to dead ends or directing you back to where you started... There is also a road that will lead you all the way through with no disruptions or distractions. You just have to be patient, consistent, have confidence, think outside the box, find your way to it and get through it.

You have to use your imagination as an outlet... Think ahead, think smart and intelligently for where there is a will there's a way and sometimes you have to get lost in order to find yourself... Identify your ability to think outside the box and put it to use.

A CHESS GAME IS A GAME OF THINKING

A CHESS MASTER ONLY MASTERS THE GAME

BY THINKING OUTSIDE OF THE BOX

=Tre Nitty Gritty=

It is an exercise for the mind that takes training and preparation. It calls for strategy, offense and defense. If you fail to calculate your moves, you can easily open up opportunities for your opponent. This could either cost you a very valuable piece or even worse the entire game and in the game of life there are no rematches.

You have to think outside the box, put yourself into your opponent's shoes, inside of their minds and think... "What would I do if I were them"? Then male your next move your best move...

IF A PERSON ONLY SEES THE OPPORTUNITIES

THAT ARE IN FRONT OF THEM THEY ARE OBLIVIOUS TO

THE OPPORTUNITIES THAT ARE SURROUNDING THEM

=Tre Nitty Gritty=

You have to improvise and have a vivid peripheral vision to visualize a way to make a way out of no way. If you can't find a way out... Find a way over, under or through. These are the =tools to become an escape artist.

Thinking outside of the box in how inventions are developed. The imagination produces miracles, this will unlock your thoughts so that you will no longer continue to be confined by limitations that will restrict you to four walls with no windows to see out of or no doors to make an exit. Do not deter from being determined, for determination and dedication take you a long way. Even when you think you are not making any progress, it could be that you are simply not "yet seeing" your progress. When you begin having thoughts of giving up, this is a very important time...   Remember that there is a must to kill the monster while it is still small or else later on down the line you will have a full-grown savage beast on your hands.

You have to take control of your thoughts and direct them to where your riches are most plentiful. Kick your thinking into overdrive and begin having =RICH SELF TALK=. Tell yourself things like "I am not a quitter", "I will not give up", Ask yourself questions related to the task or situation at hand. Do not stop until you come up with an answer or results that will bring you the best possible outcome. We have to learn how to use adversity in our favor and turn it into a benefit. Fire, flames and heat are used to test the strength of gold and are also used to mold, bend and shape steel while adversity is nature's way of testing the strength of humans, molding and forming us into strong, sharp and valuable fine pieces of work.

EVERY OBSTACLE IN LIFE IS AN OPPORTUNITY

THINK OUTSIDE THE BOX TO ESCAPE THE BOX

=Tre Nitty Gritty=

TOOL # 21

BUILD BRIDGES / DON'T BURN THEM

DO NOT BUILD A BRIDGE

THEN BURN THE BRIDGE

FOR THERE MAY COME A TIME

WHEN YOU'LL NEED TO CROSS IT AGAIN

=Tre Nitty Gritty=

Building bridges could consist of building relationships, businesses, opportunities that could open doors and lead you down a successful path in life. Bridges can get you over bumps and hurdles, through dangerous waters and across some of the deadliest of valleys. Burning a bridge that you have dedicated time, energy and finances into its design would not prove to be an intelligent decision or action on your behalf. It could prove to be a very costly mistake on many levels. Burning a bridge could be a conscious decision or an unconscious error of judgment.

MANY THINGS CAN PLAY A PART IN

THE DESTRUCTION OF YOUR OWN CONSTRUCTION

SO, BE MINDFUL OF YOUR ACTIONS.

=Tre Nitty Gritty=

There are some unspoken rules that should be upheld without the need of them being spoken, similar to the laws of the land, human nature and common sense. Things such as "do unto others as you would want done to you", "give respect to get respect", accept accountability for your actions", stand strong, behind and always keep your word", "do not speak behind peoples backs and do not allow others to do so in your presence. If you listen to people speak of negativity you are allowing them to plant negative seeds into your mind.

Know that a person who will stoop to the level of talking behind others backs will do the same to you in your absence... like the saying goes... "any dog that will bring a bone will carry one" In other words if you tell them something they are liable to go and repeat it to someone else and if they will talk to you about someone else, they will talk to someone else about you.

If they will tell you someone else's business they will have no problem spreading your business around. This alone can be the fuel to the fire of burning a very valuable bridge in your life where no form of reconstruction will be able to repair the damage.

LIFE AND DEATH ARE IN THE POWER OF THE TONGUE

YOUR OWN WORDS CAN CAUSE YOUR VERY OWN DEMISE.

=Tre Nitty Gritty=

If you ever give someone your word, be sure that you keep it. There is nothing worse than attempting to pull the wool over the eyes of an individual who places their trust in you simply by taking your word at face value. When you don't have anything else left in the world you should at least possess solid credibility, standing as a reliable individual whose word is as good as gold.

Your word could get you anything that you ask for or it could get you nothing at all. In a world where credit is king, your credit all depends on your credit history. So be sure to remain a credible individual.

You may not appreciate a lot of things until they are no longer accessible to you. You may find yourself in need of a particular person, place or thing then come to the realization that you have burned a valuable bridge or closed a very important door preventing you from gaining access to its entrance or availability.

You have to learn to recognize the value of things and respect their worth. Understand the damage that you can cause by simply doing or saying harmful things. Bridges are built to serve a purpose... Usually there is a need for the continuous use of them for the purpose of getting to and from whether in the physical world or to a goal that you have set out to achieve.

Thinking that you can use and abuse them to get where you need to be and never have to rely on them again is a form of folly. You never know what will present itself in your life that could cause you to deter and redirect you back to the very same place where you have come from, leaving you in a position of needing to cross that very same bridge once again.

Some may receive credit cards in the mail, mistake them for and "misuse" them as money. In-turn they damage a very valuable bridge before becoming aware of its worth.

The bridge of credit can be built or burned all with one signature or one swipe of a credit card.

Time proves that building a bridge securely, keeping it sturdy, maintaining its stability and ensuring that it remains operable is just as important as its initial purpose of being designed. Do not begin to neglect things when their value could be priceless.

TOOL # 22

QUALITY & QUANTITY

They say it's quality over quantity... I'd say, having a perfect balance between the two would prove to be much more valuable than just having quality alone. In the eyes of the open eyed, quality and quantity both work hand in hand. You could have something of good quality but not enough in quantity to satisfy or to even suppress the hunger or the ability to supply its demand.

You could also have a large quantity of something that lacks any quality at all whatsoever proving to be absolutely useless in fulfilling its purpose. As a Rich Thinker, your thought process should be formulating an effective plan to bring the two different components together meeting as close to the middle as possible with an ultimate goal of leading the aspect of quality over onto the quantity side of the production scale.

In doing business it's all about doing numbers... Your mission statement should reflect the goal of producing a quantity of quality work and the continuation of keeping consistent with providing top grade services. As a human being, you should strive to possess a good quantity of quality traits and live to set an example to others of how to fulfill this requirement of excellence.

Teach others, so that they are able to fit for the position or purpose as well as qualified to fit to satisfy the conditions of the detail. Develop a system of maintaining the standards of controlling the quality of your quantity. This will increase your value, secure and expand your wealth. Simply by knowing your worth, utilizing your ability to sharpen your skills. Keeping them sharp will sharpen your mind and by sharpening your mind your will sharpen your actions...

TOOL # 23

EMBRACE LOSSES

"The difference between those who fail and those who succeed are the ones who never give up."

A loss is only as big as you make it out to be. The way that you view things can either magnify or minimize the situation. You can use your losses as motivation or allow them to be your anchor to hold you back and keep you unmotivated. The choice is yours... Once you come to the realization that you are in charge of the effects that losing has over you it will open your eyes to the fact that any time you lose, you don't only lose but you also gain.

This is where you begin to turn your losses into lessons and allow those lessons to blossom into blessings. Seeing the glass as being half full instead of half empty. Do not complain about experiencing pain because without experiencing pain there would be no gain. Any "MINOR" or "MAJOR" setback is an opportunity for a "GREATER" comeback. Usually when a person is at their lowest is when their determination and drive is at its highest. Their hunger is intensified, their aggression is amplified causing them to excel and surpass any point of their expectation.

It's not about how hard you fall... It's more about how much strength you gain while you are down and how much more powerful and stronger you are once you get back up on your feet.

GIVING EVERYTHING THAT YOU HAVE

IS THE RECIPE TO GAINING EVERYTHING

THAT YOU DESIRE

It takes an energetic approach and attentive focus to see things all the way through to the end. People will only take you as seriously as you are taking yourself... So don't take yourself lightly. Take the time to experience triumph after tragedy. This will only make the success that much more intense and the impact that much more effective.

As long as you continue on without giving up you have not failed. You will only fail the moment that you throw in the towel and quit up until then you are still in the game. Some people will sit and cry over spilled milk while others recognize that "what's done is done", clean it up and keep it moving, move on and strive to not make the same mistake twice.

The struggle tends to bring our inner abilities to the surface that we unknowingly possess. When we feel like our back is against the wall our animal instincts will activate and we will fight our way out of the corner that we are backed up into.

Embrace your losses as if you are giving them a firm hug. Speak to them and give them thanks for providing you with the opportunity to experience them. Learn from them, capitalize off of them, turn them into trophies and place them on a mantle.

Reminisce, remember and reflect on them... Allow them to give you growth and development instead of hindering your progression. You have to welcome your losses wholeheartedly for they are the support to the foundation of your success... Milk them for everything that they are worth.

TOOL # 24

MONITOR YOUR PROGRESS

You could be making gradual progress and not be aware of it if you aren't frequently observing how far you have advanced from the point of where you started to your current position.

BECOME A MONITOR

OF SELF

Throughout your day, week, month and year, make it a point to stop doing whatever it is that you are doing at the moment. Take a break, sit down and conduct a SELF

ANALYZATION of your progress...... If you do not pay attention to your position, you will not know where you are standing and if you do not know where you are currently, how are you going to be able to determine the correct route of reaching your destination?

Monitor the progress that you make... Not doing so could prove to be a costly mistake. If you fail to monitor your progress you could be missing out on important points in time where you could be taking effective action. You could be possibly moving backwards... Either that or sitting stuck at a standstill unknowingly simply because you aren't monitoring your progress.

Not knowing could be preventing you from doing something about your situation, so be aware. You wouldn't want to be doing extensive work only to lose the results or to miss out on an opportunity of capitalizing off of them by failing to keep track of or knowing how much progress you have actually made.

Your awareness could prove to be the glue that holds your plans, work and success together assuring that they remain intact and inseparable from one another. Each step that you take forward constitutes a forward progression... So, keep stepping. Imagine your progress is being tracked by a machine such as a heart monitor. You have to be able to recognize the moment that you skip a beat so that you can take the necessary steps to get back on que.

Revive yourself and avoid FLATLINING... Become the actual monitoring device that is sending out the alert signals and notifications. This will ensure that you are secure on your path and prevent you from having a head on collision with failure or even a close brush with a tragic occurrence.

TOOL # 25

MULTI-FOCUSING

To focus is to have the ability to direct your attention to a particular thing or thought. Producing a very clear image whether it be something in the physical form or a vivid depiction of the imagination. Once you set a goal you will then need to conjure up a plan to achieve it. There will be a need for you to get focused and stay focused in order for you to complete the task.

You will have to be able to center your attention upon the particular area of your interest and direct a combined effort of energy and consistency towards the conquest. When driving you have to focus on the road, the vehicle that you are operating, the motorist that is traveling around you, the speed limit, street signs, traffic lights, pedestrians etc.

You have to be able to be able to focus on multiple things all at once... This will be considered the task of multi-focusing. We have to adjust our eyes until we are met with a state of clear definition. The degree of your resolution will determine the optical clarity of your sharpness. A sniper wouldn't be able to live up to their name without having the ability of multi-focusing...

This is a major contributing factor to their leverage in the field. They are armed with high caliber weapons, ammunition, scopes and sharp shooting skills but they have to use their tool of multi-focusing in order to make effective contact on their intended target. Your focus could be lying dormant... If this is so, find a way to stimulate and awaken it. Once you lock an object into your sights, zero in and remain focused.

Do not allow anything to interfere with you striking the bullseye of your target... Moving with blurred vision is along-side of moving blindly. Get focused so that you can see things crystal clear instead of seeing illusions or mistaking things for what they are not. In life we have to be able to see things in 20/20, maneuver with open eyes, never blink and stay focused.

Being able to get focused and stay focused will take a lot of strict discipline, training of the mind, mastering of emotions, temptations and reactions. Simply because there are a lot of things that can very easily become a distraction to us, disturb our focus and steal our attention even if it's only for a moment.

 That second could cost us dearly... As humans we are naturally drawn towards things that capture our interest whether it be certain sounds, colors or cravings. We cannot allow outside influences to be our masters and allow them to overpower us, re-routing our focus and placing it upon them.

You first learn to juggle by starting off juggling with two items... Once your skills begin to elevate along with your confidence, you'll add another item into the equation. Before you know it, you will have become a MASTER JUGGLER.

YOUR ATTENTION SPAN

HAS TO HAVE TO ABILITY TO

EXPAND

IN ORDER TO EXERCISE THE TASK OF

MULTI-FOCUSING

=Tre Nitty Gritty=

TOOL # 26

DEDICATION

Having dedication is a very valuable tool to possess in anything that you do. Dedication shows determination. When you are determined and dedicated to get something done, your commitment to the task will amplify your concentration and drive you to see it all the way through to completion.

Dedication is fueled by determination... Dedicate yourself to being determined and do not allow distractions to detour you. Take your life into your own hands and do not allow others to be the drivers and yourself to become a passenger of where you are headed.

Become dedicated to Thinking Rich... Utilize your imagination for everything that it is worth and think yourself all the way to success. Develop the habit of applying dedication in all that you do. Everything from asking questions, seeking information, studying, growing, thinking, planning, taking action, mastering your thoughts, completing your task, using your tools.

You have to be proactive and take the initiative towards becoming dedicated. Your devotion will tie you to your commitment and allegiance displaying the loyalty that you possess towards standing as an all-around dedicated individual.

THE VALUES THAT YOU STAND UPON

WILL STAND OUT

CLEARLY DEFINING YOUR

CHARACTER

=Tre Nitty Gritty=

A lot of times as humans we tend to begin things then later divert from finishing them. Once we come to the realization that dedication is the line that lies between complete and incomplete, success or failure, triumph or tragedy, rising or falling... We will become aware of how essential it is to be devoted and having dedication.

There are so many people who will wait until the New Year to make a commitment with themselves as if there is only a certain time of the year when making the decision to make a change in our lives is possible. They come up with a New Year's Resolution that usually lasts for either one hour, one day, one week, once a month, or in some cases maybe even one year.

In the end, if and when they backslide and revert back to their old behavior the cause is usually because they lacked the determination from the very beginning. It's easier to stay the same and continue doing what you are accustomed to doing vs making a change and beginning to do things differently.

This is why it is important that you have a substantial amount of drive behind your determination to push you forward and prevent you from giving up before you even get started.

If your goal is to lose weight do not wait until the New Year to make this commitment to yourself... Tomorrow isn't promised to any of us as individuals and the only time that you can make a change is right here right now. Make a plan on how you intend to accomplish your goal and go for it. Do intensive research on the best way for you to receive the results that you desire.

Conduct a strict SELF ANALYZATION and detect your problem areas. Once you complete your =troubleshooting=, get active and stay active... =USE YOUR TOOLS= and your dedication will drive you to your destination.

TOOL # 27

RESILIENCE

Being RESILIENT is an ABILITY

Of the BRILLIANT

=Tre Nitty Gritty=

There are times that will present themselves in our lives where we will have to have the ability of being resilient. Often people say that you should never bend, never fold or never change but truthfully at times, outside of our control we have to have the ability to transform and adapt. Having resilience gives us the power of temporarily changing our form to fit and endure any situation then resuming back to our normal selves unaffected by the trials and tribulations that we may have come to face.

A chameleon is a very small and unique reptile with the power of changing its color to adapt and blend in with its surroundings, camouflaging itself from any possible predators or imminent danger that may become prevalent. We have to be able to use our animal instincts to create a smoke screen shielding ourselves as a precaution from any threat by temporarily altering our image.

Disguising our identity by momentarily becoming a gifted chameleon misleading and creating an illusion for the eye with concealment of our true selves when becoming camouflaged is necessary. This will display our resiliency once we convert back to our original forms unaffected by any changes that we may have had to make in the face of adversity.

Do not allow situations to shape you... Shape yourself to fit into any situation, Then, utilize your ability to transform RESILIENTLY back to your original origin.

TOOL # 28

BENEFIT

The more you broaden your ability to benefit, the more beneficial you will become to yourself and others. Thinking Rich and Living Rich will open doors of opportunity. Those opportunities will come along with a lot of benefits... Also, a lot of responsibility.

You can train your brain to think of many ways to benefit. You can also train your eyes to see and recognize benefits as the present themselves.

Your mind has the ability of creating benefits that could benefit yourself and also prove to be beneficial to others. It is rare for anyone to do anything without intending to receive some sort of benefit whether it be in finances or some other form of a reward.

Their goal may be to become beneficial to others by helping out or offering some sort of service, providing aid in a particular area of requirement. By Thinking Rich and Living Rich, we ourselves BECOME a BENEFIT being that this is a way of being favorable and a helpful factor assisting with the improvement of the world and society as a whole or individuals on an individual basis.

There are benefits such as insurance that secure and insure us in many different ways such as, home owners, renters, business, property, vehicle coverage, health and life insurance policies that prove to be of benefit serving their own unique purposes in particular areas of our lives.

Usually, these benefits call for a deposit and or a recurring payment along with a negotiated contract agreement benefiting financially for the providers of the service in a sense of scratch my back and I'll scratch your back form of protection for us as the consumers.

The things that you read, watch on television, listen to in music, practice personally or indulge in could either be of a benefit or prove to not be of any benefit at all. It takes you to stay alert and aware, by using your ability to recognize a benefit vs something that will not be any benefit and refrain from partaking in anything that would be a waste of your valuable time.

You should strive to receive a benefit with anything that you invest your time into. If you are reading a book "of any kind" Find some sort of message or useful information within it. Instead of just reading or looking over something... Read through it and look into it until you locate something of value.

THERE IS ALWAYS GOLD IN THE MIND

YOU JUST HAVE TO DIG DEEP

AND FIND IT WITHIN THE GOLDMINE OF

YOUR THOUGHTS

=Tre Nitty Gritty=

TOOL # 29

REMAIN HUMBLE

MOVE HUMBLY THROUGHOUT LIFE

OR LIFE WILL FIND ITS OWN WAY TO

HUMBLE YOU

=Tre Nitty Gritty=

You can work hard for days, months or years before finally achieving a desired level of success. A lot of times going from having nothing to having plenty can cause some people to feel and ultimately act differently. In life, change is very necessary but what we have to do as Rich Thinkers, is assure that the changes that we make are for the better.

Do not allow money, material things or success to change you into or become a malice, arrogant, selfish, cocky, inconsiderate, conceited, self-centered, uppity individual for just as you gained, anything that you possess you could easily lose it all. Easy come / Easy go. Things can disappear quicker and easier than you acquired them, they say that it's lonely at the top but it's even lonelier when you work your way all the way to the top, abuse your power and success then fall and land back at the bottom.

Karma is real... Whether or not you receive good or bad karma all depends on your actions. The energy that you choose to put out into the universe will determine your fate. This is why it is important to spread love, health, wealth, riches, positivity and growth to our fellow peers and provide our youth with fruitful ways of becoming successful.

If you release negative energy out into the universe you will receive negative results in return. There may be a time when you will "ACT" first before thinking or even "THINK" the "WRONG THOUGHTS" then act on those negative thoughts producing negative actions and bringing forth a negative outcome.

"We are what we THINK, for what we THINK, we will DO" ... Like the saying goes... "If you knew better, you'd do better" so THINK RICH & LIVE RICH. People will stoop to living a lower level of a life becoming what some people would label as being a low life. They will rob. Lie, steal or kill to get the things that they desire.

They thrive off of taking from the ones who have worked hard to earn what they possess. They took the necessary steps to arrive where they are in life only to fall victim to someone's evil mind that is traveling through life along the devil's highway of darkness. At times, this immediate gratification will place blindfolds over the eyes of these evildoers. The feeling of receiving money or material items can be an illuminating bright light blinding them from seeing clearly.

Some of these evildoers may even reach a certain level of success but eventually "KARMA" will present itself right when they least expect it. It's just the laws of human nature...

WHAT GOES AROUND

COMES AROUND

SO, BE MINDFUL OF WHAT YOU

THROW AROUND

=Tre nitty gritty=

A lot of times it may come right when these particular individuals have decided to change their lives and attempt to live righteously. The same fruit that once tasted so sweet on their lips they have now become on the taste buds and in the eyes of the other like minded individuals whose motives are similar or may be even worse than theirs once was.

Be mindful of how you go about treating people on the day-to-day for those same people who you step on may have you underneath their shoe some day and what you do now could dictate what they will do once the shoe is on the other foot. This is why it is important to help others and do as much good as you possibly can... Of course, there is always the possibility of bad things coming our way but the all-seeing and all-knowing GOD is the ALMIGHTY MASTER and will be our PROTECTOR from evil.

If such shall arrive at our door steps and we are to fall victim to circumstance we have to realize that we are all just a small part of a much larger picture. In other words, the world is much bigger than us and the things that take place on this earth are all a part of GOD's plan. Regardless of how you are living in life be sure that you are moving humbly and that you always remain humble for the meek shall inherit the earth.

TOOL # 30

EVOLVE

YOU HAVE TO BE AN EVOLUTIONIST

IN ORDER TO BE EVOLVABLE

IN THE PROCESS OF

EVOLVEMENT

Evolving is a natural process that is necessary for furthering the development of the mind, expanding your business and or any other area of life that calls for growth. As the world evolves, so must we as humans. It is a part of our original origin from birth. The unfolding of events that are changing from earlier forms is the result of EVOLUTION.

Change will come... Willingly or Unwillingly. Whether you accept it or not, the body will change as you age. Some may experience the graying of their hair while others will lose their hair as it begins to become thin. You may begin to notice tension developing within your joints when attempting to complete certain tasks. You could be one who exercises regularly and your body may be in great exterior condition but the slightest move could affect something on the interior and cause aches, pains or possibly severe damage.

Noticing these things will call for us to evolve and begin to think ahead, take extra precaution and move accordingly to how our bodies are functioning. If you do not take it upon yourself to make a change... The universe will change your circumstances. You have to change something about yourself for the betterment of you. Wouldn't you rather be in control of your change instead of some unforeseen outside force?

Grow, expand your mind and exercise your talents. A gradual change is progression, a step forward into the light and the direction of evolving.

USE YOUR IMAGINATION

TO CREATE NEW LIFE

OPPORTUNITIES

=Tre Nitty Gritty=

You have to have a successful vision in your mind's eye. If you can't see yourself being successful you are destined for failure. Success begins and ends with you and your own beliefs. What you believe "IS" or "ISN'T" possible will become your only obstacle. What you believe is usually wherever your fate lies... In other words, your fate lies in your faith.

Have faith in your ability to make a change, your power to make things happen and your gift to do great things. We all have a particular source of energy that we can use in our favor. By applying it into a certain direction where we will receive the most positive result, we can achieve a level of greatness in our lives that is well beyond our imagination.

You have to magnify the capacity of your mind by opening it up and filling it with positive information, inspirational thoughts and motivational dialect. Once you acquire this enormous amount of information and vocabulary there will be a need to exercise your knowledge and skill on an effective platform.

Your word-play and delivery has to be applied in the most effective manner. Words have power...   So much power that you can truly speak things into existence. Therefore, be sure that your thoughts and words are directed towards anything that will assist you with your self-evolvement.

As History shows... Words stand to exist longer than any form of life. This is why it is important to know what you say, write, create or develop will have an impact on your life in the now and on the lives of others who are yet to come. Even in your physical absence, your words can have a long-lasting effect and continue to be a powerful contributing factor on the future evolution of the world so, EVOLVE and continue EVOLVING.

TOOL # 31

CONQUER YOUR FEARS

FEAR IS A FACTOR THAT COULD EITHER

CAUSE US TO FAIL

OR

PUSH US TO PREVAIL

=Tre Nitty Gritty=

It is a must that you recognize your fears, address and conquer them... All fears are conquerable. A fear is simply a blockage that lingers around inside of the imagination along with All of the other "WHAT IF's". As with many other things in life your fears begin and end with you. They only have as much power over you that you allow them to have. The longer you continue to breathe life into them the longer they will exist.

Once you come to conquer your fears you will become fearless. A lot of people have a fear of the UNKNOWN... Even though the unknown is completely outside of our control, we still have the ability to conquer the fear of not knowing by coming to understand that this fear is simply a state of mind. Anything that exist on the inside of our minds we have the ability of dominating by having   =RICH SELF TALK= Say to yourself, repeatedly...

1. I am a CONQUEROR.

2. I fear no one or NO THING.

3. I can conquer ALL.

4. I am FEARLESS!

There are a lot of different things that people have a fear of... Some fear heights, roller coaster rides, stepping outside of their comfort zone, animals, swimming, change, rejection, failure, aging, being alone, living, dying etc... The best way to overcome your fears is to face them head on. If you are afraid of heights, get on an airplane and take a flight, look out of the window once you are thousands of miles high into the sky. Get comfortable, relax and embrace your victory.

A lot of things are not actually all that bad... They are only as bad as we depict them in our thoughts. If you have a fear of being alone, go somewhere, seclude yourself and sit in silence. This is a way to become closer and more familiar with yourself. A time to enjoy peace, quiet and tranquility.

If you are in fear of death you have to interrupt that pattern and way of thinking. Replace those fears with courage and look at death as a graduation... A time to celebrate life instead of a mournful time of grief and sorrow. Understand that you have no control over when or how you are going to depart from this world. I suggest that you get right with God and have faith that all will take place on his time for his time is the only right time.

There is no need to LIVE in fear of DEATH for DEATH is simply a part of LIFE... Once we are born there is no way of getting around dying. Once you decide to face your fears you have taken the first step towards conquering them. Get your emotions under control and steer clear of panic and or distress for they are simply a development that has grown inside of our minds caused by the expectation of pain.

Throughout life in many ways, we will be exposed to danger and possibly have a few close encounters with death. That does not mean that we have to live in fear of harm. When we fear any little thing, it gives outside influences power and the ability to control us. Take a moment to calm yourself and breathe easy. This will lower your anxiety before it rises to a level that could possibly drive you into a state of panic.

Embrace nervousness and the feeling of fear. Curve your reaction and redirect its energy towards assisting you instead of allowing it to cripple you. Our strong minds have the power to overthrow our weak minds. It's all about the area of where you apply your strength on the balancing scale of your thoughts of whether you will LIVE IN FEAR or LIVE WITHOUT FEAR.

Thinking Rich will drive you to crush, subdue, defeat and deliver you from being afraid or having fear lingering around through your mind and heart. Conquer your fears instead of allowing them to conquer you.

HAVING FEAR WON'T GET YOU

ANYWHERE

FEARING NOTHING YOU CAN GO

TOOL # 32

CAPITALIZE

Capitalizing is making a strong and bold effort that produces large results. Taking advantage of any given situation creating an opportunity out of a possibility. In relation to the alphabet, you have capital letters vs small letters. Capital letters are used to instill a strong and bold effect into the minds of the readers by grabbing their attention in a superior way over lower-case letters serving their purpose of capitalization.

The wise minded will capitalize and take advantage of all opportunities. Make an achievement and advance from their current position while striving to reign supreme with their progression. Once you gain momentum, keep the ball rolling, become adhesive with your plans and stick to them.

When lacking the "stick-to-it-ness" we will often lose our grips and begin to slip due to the lack of traction to the surface upon which we stand. You have to capitalize off of each one of your abilities. In order to complete this task you must have an open mind, open eyes and the gift to recognize an opportunity for what it is.

There are many capabilities that we possess yet we tend to take them for granted instead of putting them to work for us such as, listening, learning and understanding. As long as we are willing to listen there are things that we can LEARN and in turn come to UNDERSTAND how to take those same LEARNINGS and begin TEACHING them to others.

Our ability to SEE gives us an opportunity next to those who are not as fortunate to have sight. Our ability to SPEAK provides us with the opportunity and the POWER to INFLUENCE others with our words. What we choose to do with this power and influence will determine our results. The mission is to spread RICH THINKING resulting in RICH LIVING by influencing others to become their RICH-SELVES.

Being able to stand on our own two feet and having the ability to walk or to run is a blessing all within itself being that there are others who struggle to simply stand and others who do not even have the option due to injuries they've sustained or disabilities that prevent them from doing so.

THE MOMENT THAT YOU RECOGNIZE

A CHANCE TO ADVANCE

IS THE CHANCE OF A LIFETIME

AND A TIME TO

CAPITALIZE

=Tre Nitty Gritty=

TOOL # 33

SELF HEALING

When you are feeling down, the only way for you to get up is to take it upon yourself to pick yourself up. You can only depend on you to accomplish this task. Remember that nobody or nothing outside of you has more power or control over how you feel on the inside. Some people may turn to drugs and or alcohol only to find that these vices are only a temporary fix. Once these chemicals wear off your reality resurfaces.

In fact, at times these psychedelics often intensify your issues stirring your emotions, elevating them to a higher level of an unbearable pain. Someone may attempt to assist you with lifting your head but no one can actually lift and hold your head up "but you" no matter how hard they may try. If you are not willing to put forth the effort your head will continue to hang low.

Do not dwell on negative things or thoughts that keep you stuck in a negative space. You can either think your way into a living hell and find yourself lost in a nightmare or you can think your way to success by continuing to Think Rich. Brainstorm on ways to achieve greatness even when times appear to be not so appealing. Life has its ups and downs, as with anything else.

You just have to be able to find your balance then stand strong and firm. If you fail to do so you will be offset and without balance you will fall, over and over again, find yourself attempting to get back up then once you struggle your way back to your feet if you continue to fail at standing you will continue to collapse.

If someone has done something to you in the past and you are busy holding onto ill feelings or resentment this will cloud your mind, ultimately causing your thoughts to not be pure and rich. Therefore, you will have to reach deep down inside, find a way to HEAL YOURSELF and forgive even if you are not able to forget.

It is understood that there are some things that just cannot be erased but at the same time you cannot waste valuable time out of your life dwelling on something or someone that isn't worth devoting a second of your thoughts upon when you could be placing your thoughts elsewhere, somewhere of more importance.

Entertaining these negative thoughts will only add fuel to the fire that is burning you up on the inside, forcing you to RELIVE these situations over and over again. You have to cut or break loose from the strings that are holding you hostage to these feelings and emotions or else they will continue to be your puppet master.

Take control of the power that this person is possessing over you. If you fail to do this, then these feelings will keep you ill and prevent your wounds from healing. They will continue to hold you stuck in the past. You will not be able to move forward freely or as easily with this ball and chain connected to your negative experiences, thoughts of life and or the people who have caused you heartbreak and pain.

People will disappoint you more often than never. You will experience situations that will steer you to begin viewing some people, places and things differently. Knowing this and being prepared for it can get you past and through particular situations as they present themselves in your life. Expect things to be somewhat complicated at times, for without trials and tribulations there will be no triumph.

If you are prepared to face these things it is less likely that they will devastate you if and when they happen to occur. Having the ability to heal yourself is aligned along with many of the tools of Think Rich / Live Rich. You have to =CLEANSE THE MIND=, have =RICH-SELF-TALK=, =EMBRACE YOUR LOSSES=, turn your losses into lessons and =CAPITALIZE== off of your abilities of doing so.

What doesn't kill you makes you stronger... Your scars and HEALED wounds will tell your story without the need or assistance of words, so HEAL YOURSELF and REBUILD YOURSELF.

TOOL # 34

FIND YOUR MOTIVATION

IN ORDER TO GET ANYWHERE, YOU WILL HAVE TO FIRST

KNOW WHERE YOU ARE GOING

=Tre Nitty Gritty=

Find what motivates YOU and sparks YOUR interest, allow it to push you towards reaching your destination. There are a lot of opportunities in the world for you to take advantage of. It's all about finding YOUR niche, YOUR area of desire. Something that grabs and holds your attention.

Possibilities are endless... You just have to be able to see past your own nose. Your thoughts will produce your future so get busy thinking, plotting, planning and taking action. There are many ways for you to seek information on whatever it is that you may have a particular interest in.

These days we are in the information age. Anything that we may want to find whether it be a person, place or a thing... It is all in the palms of our hands or at the tips of our fingers. The abilities of today's technology are endless. It can take us to unimaginable heights. Cellular phones and other electronics such as laptops / computers or anything that has a Google (search) engine that can open many doors for us.

We may not have had the luxury or the opportunity of exploring these experiences if it weren't for the creators that are responsible for Thinking Rich and Living Rich.... They developed these incredible systems and devices that assist us in so many ways in our lives today. They provide us with ways and avenues to create great things for the future and make changes in our lives that can change the lives of others.

There are many things that were once kept away and hidden from us in places where we may have never had access to that are now available to us upon our demand. The simple click of a button or even something as simple as asking a question through voice recognition can give us directions, resources and connections, answers on history, politics or anything else that we may conjure up, from the simplest thing to the most complex and complicated.

What we choose to do with this high-quality information source will determine our results. "We, ourselves, are the only obstacle that can stand in our way.

DO NOT BLOCK YOUR OWN PATH

&

DO NOT LIMIT YOURSELF

Use social media for more than just socializing... Utilize it to Build Networks / Friendships. Remember the mission is to USE YOUR TOOLS... Always strive to Capitalize and Benefit. With this giant monster, we have the ability of becoming global, international corporations capitalizing off of all corporate benefits. We can start from scratch, build a small business then turn that small business into a gigantic empire. All it takes is for you to FIND YOUR MOTIVATION, BOSS UP, GET ACTIVE / STAY ACTIVE and USE YOUR TOOLS.

We have the opportunity to sell ideas, information, food, clothes, homes, vehicles, services, books, movies, music, arts & entertainment, electronics, etc. There is no limit to what we can do or how far we can go in life. The only limits that we will face are the ones that we place upon ourselves. At times it may take us seeing certain things in-order for our eyes to become open to them. Seeing is believing, so seeing is a good way to awaken our desires or gain our attention, bringing us to the realization that we have an interest in whatever it may be.

If you are motivated by success, money or having long lasting wealth... You should study the things that millionaires and billionaires did in order to obtain their level of riches and "MOST IMPORTANTLY" what they do to "KEEP" them. Master their ways and incorporate them into your own plans in an order that they will work for you. This will lead you in the direction that you are heading with guidance while learning from and avoiding the mistakes that were made by the ones before you... At the same time FINDING YOUR MOTIVATION...

BECOME A MIXTURE OF MASTER-MINDS

AND YOU WILL BECOME THE ULTIMATE

MASTER-MIND

=Tre Nitty Gritty=

Once you find your motivation and decide the path that you wish to travel in life you will be able to begin your journey towards accomplishing your goals. You can become a living example whom others can turn to when looking for motivation, information, instruction and direction. This is an area of life where there are many people who are in need of assistance. Proper or improper guidance could prove to be the difference between success and failure.

Use the world wide web "www." to research any and everything that you can imagine from motivational speakers, life coaches and "how-to" videos or various subjects from building businesses, accounting, managing, intellectual property, real-estate, patents, copyrights, trademarks etc. For the more you know the more you can reiterate for the masses.

Find what motivates you and do not draw the line at the minimum. Instead, strive to be a wearer of many hats, a person with a plethora of skills, make them benefit your life and the lives of others simultaneously. Once your motivational spark is ignited, keep it lit and never allow it to fizzle out.

TOOL # 35

PRIORITIZE

PRIORITIZE AND ORGANIZE

THIS WILL BENEFIT YOU

MORE THAN YOU REALIZE

=Tre Nitty Gritty=

Prioritizing your life will give you a firm and solid ground to build and stand upon. Once you come to terms of what's most important, you will begin putting first things first and getting things finished in an organized manner. Everything in life has a particular order of importance but at times they will tend to bleed outside the lines of organization.

We have to be the judges and decide what holds the most presidency amongst our to do list. This does not make the "less-relevant", "Irrelevant" They may still be necessary tasks to complete, it's just that by prioritizing you will first take care of the most urgent things of primary importance. If you do not prioritize your values, your responsibilities will be scattered all over the place.

You have to know what things are most important, not only just to you personally for at times our emotions can attempt to lead us to believe that something is more important than it actually is. Times like these we have to remember that we are the masters of our emotions. We have to maintain control and not allow our emotions to do our decision making for us.

You will first have to know the importance of your values in order for you to have the ability to prioritize them. Once you come to understand the differentiating weight of your values you will be better able to determine their necessary placement. Make a commitment to being a prioritized individual for moving without prioritization you are moving without structure. You will have to ask yourself questions like...

1. WHO are the most important people in my life?

2. WHAT are my responsibilities?

3. WHEN and what do I need to do first?

4. WHERE and how am I going to get it done?

5. WHY are these values important and how much weight do they hold?

Throughout life you will hear people state the phrase "Get your priorities straight" In other words this means to get yourself organized.

GET YOUR PRIORITIES IN ORDER

FOR ANYTHING WITHOUT ORDER

IS OUT OF ORDER

=Tre Nitty Gritty=

TOOL # 36

EXPRESS YOURSELF

Make a strong representation of who you are as a person. Make it clear and unmistakable known what it is that you stand for. If you do not stand for something you will fall for anything and if you will fall for anything you will not stand for nothing. With words along with your actions you can express yourself defiantly and directly to those of whom you wish to target with your expressions.

There are rules, laws, rights and beliefs that we must stand up for and behind in order for them to hold any validity in the order of the world. When it comes to anything of value, once the backing diminishes the value depreciates. If a bank account is holding a large amount of money, it is holding value and is valuable.

If for whatever reason the money is to disappear the value of that bank account would decrease. Same way with us as human beings... If we do not express ourselves, what we value will hold no merit. Find a way to express yourself or you will naturally begin storing and bottling things up on the inside creating pounds of pressure that could possibly become deadly for yourself and others.

Expressing yourself is a tool to vent, serving as an outlet done by the making of a statement whether it be in your body language, the clothes you wear, verbal or communicating through signs and symbols.

This will bring you a sense of freedom... A feeling of relief from a state of being heard. If you do not speak up for yourself, who is going to speak up for you? In order to get your point across you have to utilize your ability to make an effective, clear and valid delivery of words and the skills of painting a vivid picture that will open the mind's eye of others. It takes a lot of heart along with having the ability to overpower your fears. If you allow your nervousness to prevent you from expressing yourself and confronting issues that you feel are in need of being addressed then you will not reach your desired point of clarification.

For many years the practice of protesting has been a tool used for expressing oneself. Coming together and standing together for a righteous cause. Demonstrating unity has brought forth justification in many different areas in shaping the world today. This form of expression has proven to be highly effective though at times some may lose sight of the sole purpose often resulting in rioting and looting but Thinking Rich and Living Rich expressing yourself would consist of the practice of positive and peaceful protesting.

YOUR EXPRESSIONS

WILL BECOME YOUR REFLECTION

SO, BE CONSCIOUS

OF YOUR MIRROR IMAGE

=Tre Nitty Gritty=

TOOL # 37

CONSISTENCY

Consistency is a very valuable tool to possess in your toolbox. It will assist you with any task that you are in the process of completing. You have to be consistent and avoid allowing interruptions to interfere with you reaching your goals or accomplishing your task. At the point when you become inconsistent it will become apparent. You will have to grasp the ability to take notice in your shift from consistent to inconsistent in order for you to be able to make the proper corrections that it will take for you to get back on track.

Being consistent shows responsibility... Once you focus on constantly being consistent it will organically become a part of your character. You can be known for constantly being inconsistent or you can build a solid reputation for being consistent in a positive and productive light. You have to remain focused and continue proceeding with a timely receptiveness. If you are hammering away at something and it seems that you aren't getting anywhere at all. This is not the time to give up. You may in fact be making plenty of progress but lack the ability of seeing it from the view where you are standing. You will have to reposition yourself in order to see things from a different angle, then continue taking swings at it.

Usually, people will give up on their dreams, plans and goals just as they are on the brink of success. Do not throw in the towel, tap out and call it quits. Keep going strong, swing steady and keep it consistent. Your consistency will pay off.

TOOL # 38

EFFECTIVE THINKING

Effective thinking is producing thoughts that will have a powerful and effective impact. Why would one spend their time thinking if their thoughts didn't enrich their position in life in some way shape or form? Take advantage of our intelligence as human beings for we are gifted with the power to create and produce things that all start from an imaginary thought inside of our minds followed up with action.

YOU WILL ONLY GO AS FAR

AS YOU THINKING WILL TAKE YOU

USE EFFECTIVE THINKING AS A POWER TOOL

AND DRILL UNTIL YOU STRIKE IT RICH

INTELLECTUALLY

=Tre Nitty Gritty=

All of your thoughts will have an effect on you in one way or another... The thing to think about is HOW they will affect you. Will the results be EFFECTIVE or INEFFECTIVE? If they are effective, will they be strongly effective in a POSITIVE or in a NEGATIVE? Our thoughts are the foundation in which we build upon. This is why THINKING RICH comes before LIVING RICH.

You have to feed your thoughts, exercise them and continue keeping them at work. Think positive and remain on a quest towards greater living and greater things. Enough is never enough when it comes to information and knowledge for knowledge is power and power is strength. So, exercise your thoughts and get intellectually fit.

When you have strong thoughts, follow them up with strong action and you will witness first-hand the effects of EFFECTIVE THINKING. There is a method and a process to thinking effectively. A cause and an effect / an action and a reaction. The cause is the initial point of what brings us to a particular thought. The effect is the action that follows that thought.

Reacting effectively to effective thinking is the equation between the two elements of effective action which is THINKING RICH and LIVING RICH.

TOOL # 39

MORALS AND PRINCIPLES

WITHOUT MORALS

ONE IS WITHOUT PRINCIPLES TO STAND UPON

=Tre Nitty Gritty=

The rules and standards of human behavior are founded upon moral law. Our conscience pokes at us anytime that we think, attempt to or partake in the act of any wrongdoing. We know when something is right and when something is wrong. We also possess the power to make the decision of doing either or. We feel good and experience good vibes when doing good deeds for others. We also are aware of the feeling we get when we begin to entertain the thought of indulging in the act of deceiving others. When this happens it is impossible to enjoy the rewards that we reap from our actions simply because our morals and principles make it difficult to overlook the dishonorable conduct in which we have delivered to obtain them.

We have to have values, standards, morals and principles that we uphold to a high enough standard where they cannot be lowered or got anything of a lesser ethical habit or value. Your integrity is something that is very important to hold onto. Losing touch from standing firm on your moralistic responsibilities will steer you into an area of life that is filled with bad karma and complete darkness.

Remaining one with your integrity is maintaining the wholeness and completeness of one's self. Going against the laws of human nature, jeopardizing and losing your integrity is the separation between you and a defiant law of nature that will in-turn serve as a defamation of character.

IF YOUR MORALS AND PRINCIPALS

ARE OFF CENTERED

THEN YOUR POINT OF VIEW

IS IN NEED OF SHIFTING

=Tre Nitty Gritty=

By shifting your view point you will begin to see things differently. This attitude adjustment will change your focus and intensify your awareness for the betterment of your moral standing. With this you will find yourself upholding the personal code of conduct for humanity. Be motivated by being morally centered and principally grounded.

TOOL # 40

CONFIDENCE

Confidence is a necessity and a must have in order to prevail through ups and downs, surpass and plow ourselves through roadblocks and Delima's. It is also needed to recover from setbacks and overcome insecurities. There is a line that lies between HAVING confidence and LACKING confidence. The range of separation between the two depends on the amount of doubt that one places upon themselves.

A lot of us tend to have more confidence in one area of life than another. The goal is to become well rounded and completely confident in every aspect. Some of us may be in need of confidence BOOSTERS... These boosters may come in a variety of different forms but in any shape that they present themselves, they can assist us with getting in tune with our confident sides.

Things like supportive comments, encouraging words, motivational suggestions, spiritual lifting and emotional building. These are all ways of instilling courage and building confidence. It may seem that some others possess more of a natural ability to complete certain tasks easier than others. This only makes things appear to be more complex to one who has to put forth more effort.

It takes intense training, conditioning, dedication and drive to become an OVERACHIEVER. This doesn't just happen overnight. You have to be willing to put one foot forward and complete the step-by-step process. Most of all... You will have to come to terms of having confidence in yourself. You are capable of becoming a master of anything that you desire. You just have to find the willpower to master the PROCESS.

Your confidence will have to be founded upon a strong foundation. Your belief in yourself will determine whether or not you will go the distance. Lacking confidence, you could kill your dreams long before they even come to life. You have to first develop a winning mentality. Then have enough trust in yourself where you become secure in your reliance. Be confident that others can have confidence in you. Have faith in your fearlessness... Be bold, courageous, positive and stand firm within your confidence.

It all begins from within... The more in-tune that you become with your inner-being the more it will reflect from your outer self. A small grain of confidence is better than no confidence at all. It gives you something to build upon. Find it and continue building.

TOOL # 41

SACRIFICE

There will come a time in the process of growth from living your unhealthy life to a life of thinking rich and living rich when you will have to make sacrifices of certain things in order to gain possession of others of richer value. We have to cut loose from some of our old habits that have done more holding us back than pushing us forward or benefiting us.

Things can be more harmful to us than helpful, yet and still we will allow these things to continue being a part of our lives overlooking the fact that they are being a hindrance in our development. Once you begin weighing your options, recognizing the worth of your values and what's most important you will begin making more wise decisions over foolish ones.

A SACRIFICE MUST BE MADE

WHEN IT COMES DOWN TO

A LIFE LOST

VS

A LIFE SAVED

=Tre Nitty Gritty=

If you are walking across a frozen river and the ice begins to crack due to an extra amount of weight that you are carrying putting your life in jeopardy. Would you choose to hold onto that extra weight or make the decision to sacrifice it in exchange for your own survival regardless of how valuable you feel it is to you at the time?

Life is filled with choices and decision making that will dictate and determine our future. If we place our lives and futures into the hands of others it is a high possibility that we may become a sacrifice of their very own. Bad habits are no different than bad company... The two are one in the same. If we continue to devote ourselves to them, entertain them and allow them to be a part of our lives we are submitting ourselves to likely becoming a sacrifice.

In order to continue thriving and elevating to new heights, growing and expanding our minds, our worlds and experiencing new opportunities we have to know when it is time to move on, time to make a decision, a change, a time to be silent and a time to speak. When it is time to make a separation, when it is time to make new connections, when it is time to make a sacrifice that will change our lives for the better. When it is time to sit our pride to the side and sacrifice it for a more worthy and valuable cause.

TOOL # 42

LIVE AND LEARN

TO LIVE IS TO BE ALIVE

THOUGH MOST WHO ARE ALIVE

FAIL TO LIVE

=Tre Nitty Gritty=

We have to recognize life's lessons for what they are. If we fail to take notice of them, they will simply go over our heads. Similar to when someone attempts to give us a valuable piece of information and instead of storing it into our mental rolodex, we allow it to flow into one ear and out of the other.

Leering is a part of growth, so in order to grow we must learn. We have to live and learn in order for us to have the ability to teach. Do not miss out on valuable information simply because you have a head that is harder than concrete and you are more stubborn than a mule.

GOING THROUGH LIFE

WITHOUT LEARNING ALONG THE WAY

IS NOT A LIFE WORTH LIVING

=Tre Nitty Gritty=

Paying attention can prove to pay off at a time when we least expect it to. You may believe that you won't need to know a particular thing for it has no relevance in your current life. At some point in time, you may find yourself in a situation where you will regret not learning or storing certain information into your memory for it could possibly save your life or the life of another.

For instance... There may have been a point in time when you were offered the opportunity of learning the process of applying CPR... At the time you may have said to yourself... "I do not have any plans on entering the medical field." Then find yourself someday in the company of a family member, friend or a complete stranger who finds themself in a life-or-death situation and in the need of being resuscitated.

If you failed to receive and learn this lesson at the time that it was offered to you then it is highly like;y that you will not have the slightest idea of where to even begin. This will be a point of no return where instead of being helpless you could have been helpful. You may wish that you had done something different but regretting not doing so will not help or change your current situation. This is why we have to live and learn along the way. Keep your mind open being that any piece of information could prove to be a lesson worth learning at some point in time, later on down the line.

TOOL # 43

PLAN YOUR ACTION

An action planned is an action well thought out with strategic strategy to execute it with perfection. Planning your action raises the potential of any plan for if you fail to plan, you plan to fail. The simplest things in life shouldn't go without planning, let alone the more complicated ones. Thought should be placed behind any action before an action is made for thought gives you direction and without direction you are without a route to lead you to your destination.

Being that your actions breed results and are the foundation of whether or not you accomplish your plans. This alone should be reason enough for you to put as much thought into your plans as possible before you put your plans into action.

The element of surprise is one of the most known forms of planning your action. You are planning your plot and plotting your plan to attack while the sleep has their eyes closed. Catching them by surprise while you are fully aware, with a well thought out plan gives you an immeasurable amount of leverage. An advantage at conquering the situation and steering the results of the outcome in your favor. The best way to strike an intended target is through planning, practice and perfection... This is how you become the executioner.

When someone decides to start a business, the first step into the process is to develop a business plan. This plan will detail the ins and outs of how this company will be conducting its operations. Within this business plan there will be a PLAN OF ACTION... which will consist of four things.

1. The mission statement: This will be the grounds of the company's mission, responsibilities and obligations.

2. The business description section: This is where the company will describe their competitive edge by painting a vivid picture for the imagination of how they will overthrow their competition.

3. The Business Marketing Plan: explaining how they will be targeting their niche area of business and marketing to potential customers.

4. The Scope of Operations: Which will cover a wide range of functions from dealing with employees to purchasing from vendors to maintaining the companies account records and financial management plan.

This plan stands to be the most valuable asset to any business startup for the plan is the road map that will guide and lead you to your destination. Many will attempt to skip this process and avoid making a plan finding every excuse under the sun as to why they don't need one. Either it's too much work, takes too much time, effort, or they simply believe that they can do just fine without it.

A lot of people only view a business plan as a tool to seek and find funding for their company, not realizing that this is how disaster strikes... Diving into a river without the thought of planning and preparing for the possibility of swimming upon a current could prove to be a costly mistake when you could have simply taken precaution to avoid a great tragedy.

PLANNING YOUR ACTION

IS THE TRAIT OF A

MASTERMIND

This is how you develop a master plan. The actions are planned and placed in a distinctive order throughout the blueprint. Within its designing is where all of the value remains. The plan is the gold and its weight is in its merit. Plan first then follow your plan up with a plan of action.

TOOL # 44

OPEN EYES / OPENS DOORS

Having sight, plus vision provides us with an ability to open doors for ourselves and others. This is a gift and a blessing that we all need to appreciate the value of having the opportunity to utilize. Possessing a set of functioning eyes provides us with sight. Having A VISION is something that is formulated from a combination of thoughts and imagination.

We can bring things into a clear view of the mind so vivid that in turn in can be developed into a tangible item or asset once we come to the point of creating things that can have an impact to the point where they will leave an imprint in the universe that will forever have our signature on it long after we are gone.

As long as our eyes are closed, we will continue to remain sleepy and blind to opportunities, failing to notice when flourishing situations present themselves. We need to open our eyes in order to have the ability to take notice of a door that is available to us before we are able to open it. Not paying attention to what is going on around us could cost us dearly whether it be financially, physically or mentally. Being ignorant is ignoring and being oblivious will serve us no justice at all.

Search for eye openers in everything that you do, whether it be in what you read, what you watch on tv or in the music that you listen to.

ANYTHING THAT YOU ALLOW

TO ENTER YOUR BRAIN

THROUGH YOUR EYES, OR YOUR EARS

WILL BECOME A PART OF YOU

=Tre Nitty Gritty=

Strive to pave roads and open doors for others along the way by creating job opportunities, passing along valuable knowledge and information. Going to the extreme when it comes to finding gold and diamonds then spreading the wealth amongst others of the community for simply holding onto and keeping all to yourself would be selfish and is not a form of living rich. You have to show your appreciation for the blessings that you receive.

Once your eyes become open to the ways of the world the more of a chance you will stand to survive in the face of society. Things will become clearer and begin to make more sense. You will realize and come to a better understanding of why things happen and how they happen, when they happen. Open your eyes and realize that nothing, no surprise shall come outside of what you have already visualized.

KNOWLEDGE BRINGS YOU WISDOM

WISDOM BRINGS YOU UNDERSTANDING

AND UNDERSTANDING GIVES YOU CLARITY

=Tre Nitty Gritty=

TOOL # 45

BEING BROKE VS BEING BROKEN

Being BROKE financially is something that can be fixed by working and doing something about your financial standing... Being BROKEN as an individual is an entirely different complex dilemma. There is a difference in a person being broke as in their financial state of being vs... an individual who is broken well beyond repair in their state of humanity.

If they are lacking the will power, drive, confidence, fearlessness, determination, courage, self-discipline, perseverance and the conditioning that it takes to avoid making excuses and coming up with reasons why they can't do certain things. They will talk themselves out of attempting to make any progress and deter from even exercising the thought of doing anything that will elevate them to a higher level of living.

If you lack the ability of thinking positive and thinking rich, how would you expect to reach the next level of living positive and living rich? You can only expect to reach the next level by climbing the ladder and taking the steps to get there, not by remaining on the same floor with your feet planted in the same position. You have to take the first step first before you even attempt to take the second... You cannot skip steps in the process.

 You may have friends or family members who you would rather not see in a bind or doing bad. Even when you are in a position with not much to offer you may still extend your hand in an attempt to pull them out of a rut. Hurting yourself in an attempt to help them by attaching yourself to them and their struggle when they are not even searching for a way out of it themselves. With this you are becoming a part of the problem instead of a part of the solution.

YOU CANNOT PASS THE BATON

TO SOMEONE WHO IS NOT EVEN IN THE RACE

AND STILL EXPECT TO COME OUT VICTORIOUS

=Tre Nitty Gritty=

A lot of times in the process of trying to help others we can injure ourselves severely. That's just a high price that we pay for having a big heart. The key is to not allow this to turn into a suicide mission. Even though we may be willing to make the sacrifice, repeating this process over and over again can be defined by the definition of insanity... Doing the same thing over and over again but expecting different results.

As a RICH THINKER you must be mindful of the ground that you till in the preparation of starting a garden. You will have to strategically plant your seeds in an organized fashion. All things need their certain amount of space in order to grow without disturbance. There is only so much tending to your produce that you can do to assist them with their growth. The rest will be left upon them by mother nature.

Most of all... A bad seed is a bad seed and there is nothing you can do to change that. Trying to save someone from themself is like fighting an uphill battle whether it be drugs, alcohol, gambling, a nonproductive lifestyle or something that most may think is simple like, decision making. You can attempt to share your vision with others but whether or not they see things the way you see them is completely up to them.

As the saying goes... You can lead a horse to water but you can't make them drink it. Just as you can drag an addict into rehab but you can't force them to refrain from indulging in whatever their addiction may be. You cannot MAKE anyone inherit your characteristic ways, your beliefs, your thoughts, your feelings, your drive, your ambition or motivation. All you can do is spill it upon them with hopes that they will absorb it.

If they don't... Then that is your que to take notice and stop attempting to spray water through a solid iron wall. Keep your positive energy and continue spreading your positive thoughts by taking your show on the road and offering your valuable information and jewels to someone who may accept them with an open mind, eyes and ears.

TOOL # 46

MASTER YOUR EMOTIONS

YOU ARE THE MASTER-KEY

TO MASTERING YOUR EMOTIONS

=Tre Nitty Gritty=

Unlock your intelligence and in-turn you will develop into a complete masterpiece. Emotions are a very vital aspect in the events that play a major role in the molding of our lives. Our emotions are the energy that sparks our reactions and fuels our decision making. A lot of times we tend to react to our emotions without putting any thought behind our actions. Emotions do not have a brain of their own, therefore you have to always remember to imbed it into your brain that you are the responsible party that has to do the thinking for them.

When someone says that they can't help themselves from reacting a certain type of way when certain things occur, they are submitting themselves to the strength of their NEGATIVE emotions not realizing that they have more power and strength resting in their POSITIVE emotional pool. They have given up and allowed their negative emotions to drive their reactions instead of gaining control and turning a negative into a positive.

As the symbol that stands to represent NEGATIVE is flat, single, plain, lonely and is usually represented by the color of black... According to the dictionary black is a color that is known to symbolize dark, dead, unresponsiveness, the negative is no good without the positive just as the positive is no good without the negative. You have to take it upon yourself to turn that negative into a positive by adding the second line to accompany it, giving it juice, bringing life to it, transforming from black to red. There is a need for you to gain and maintain the balance and master the art of keeping your emotions under your own self-mastery.

Once you become aware of this it will become a part of your normal thought process, in turn influencing your actions with you being in full control over your decision making. Uncontrolled actions that are led by emotions can cause a chain of events to unfold that could very likely be irreversible. Becoming aware of this gives us the ability to become the masters of our emotions contrary to allowing our emotions to master us.

Our emotions can drive us into the ground... "Literally". A lot of people will become depressed for a number of different reasons and often it may seem that things happen so fast and back-to-back that it causes the pain and the weight to seem unbearable. This can drive some past the point of no return and push them to the point of losing all hope. Instead of continuing to suffer they may exercise thoughts of, attempt to or God forbid, succeed at committing suicide.

Depression is real... and is not something that should be taken lightly. Depression can break the strongest person down to their knees for the fact that being physically fit does not constitute for being emotionally fit. You have to find a way to get a grip on things, master your emotions and how you react to situations that are outside of your control while maintaining control over the things that you do have control over... Starting with YOURSELF...

As humans, we are all emotional creatures at heart... Our emotions are a very strong, mental, instinctive feeling that can be intensified by either love or fear. We have to become masters of our instincts in order to become masters of our emotions.

FOR EVERY ACTION

THERE IS A REACTION

BUT EVERY ACTION

DOES NOT DESERVE A REACTION

=Tre Nitty Gritty=

To become the MASTER is to become the OWNER who is RESPONSIBLE. Being that we are all RESPONSE-ABLE... We are able to respond INTELLIGENTLY. You have to become the captain of your own ship and have the ability, strength, knowledge, skill, endurance and perseverance to sail through deadly waters no matter what type of storm you may sail into.

You never know when a storm may come, but as long as you are strong enough to weather the storm you will survive through it. In the end... All storms will eventually come to an end. Get a grip on life and keep the upper hand. Mastering our emotions is a science and with the correct chemistry it can be done by us all. We just have to open our eyes and operate intelligently, for intelligence is always over emotions.

You will continue to suffer if you have an emotional breakdown to everything that you come to face. In life there are a lot of unfortunate things that we will encounter and be forced to deal with. Our power comes from the strength of our restraint and controlling how we react to these things. You have to become a skilled practitioner and exercise your proven ability to be masterful by acquiring complete knowledge and mastering the skill of mastering your emotions.

MASTER YOUR EMOTIONS

DO NOT ALLOW YOUR EMOTIONS

TO MASTER YOU

=Tre Nitty Gritty=

TOOL # 47

STEEL SHARPENS STEEL

JUST AS STEEL SHARPENS STEEL

WE AS HUMANS ARE BUILT WITH THE ABILITY

TO SHARPEN ONE ANOTHER

=TRE NITTY GRITTY=

In order for this to take place it takes one to possess humbleness and having the willingness to share with and accept effective information from others spreading knowledge and wisdom bringing forth understanding. We have the ability of learning from one another and sharing each other's visions. The eyes cannot see further than the mind

There are many facts that support the fact that steel sharpens steel... Such as "Great minds think alike" "Each one teaches, one" "Think together & grow together" "Teamwork makes the dreamwork". It is not about having a wrestling match or being in competition about who knows the most or who is more superior as the teacher for the fact that we can all learn from someone who we least expect to learn anything from.

There is a lot of truth in the saying that "You can learn a LOT from a DUMMY". So do not neglect the idea of learning from the mistakes of others. Also... there are people who are sharper than others in certain areas. This brings a balance to the table where we are able to build together and help each other's minds expand by strengthening and growing one another in our flawed areas.

Two minds are said to be greater than one... Especially when they are two like-minded individuals who are thinking rich and living rich. The stronger mental connection that you are able to make with someone the more voltage will run through those cables and there is no limit to the thoughts or the results that those thoughts can reach.

The more information that you allow to be driven into your brain the more you will have to offer. There are so many things to learn how to do and get familiar with that could prove to be beneficial in our lives that there should never be a dull moment, only sharp thinking and lots of improvement. A lot of times I hear people state that they are bored...

My reaction is usually "Well, maybe you should go find something to do." Being a person who can't comprehend boredom from my personal life experiences where 24 hours in a day never seems to be enough time, I cannot relate to being bored. When you become a person who is thinking rich and living rich, wearing many hats you will be so busy that the word bored will remove itself from your thought processing. When you have two or more people who share similar interest, drive, determination and motivation you will find that their chemistry usually inspires one another.

Do not allow bored people to stick around for too long being that the longer they linger around, so does their aura. If you can't get rid of them, remove yourself because eventually their boring energy will begin to take away your active energy draining you and bringing you to the less energetic level of the unmotivated leaving you amongst the bored.

Just as we have the ability to sharpen each other we can also dullen one another. This is one reason why a chess master avoids playing chess against someone who is no longer of competition to them. It begins to weaken their chess game and this could cause them to lose their competitive edge for there is no challenge and with that they don't have to use their creative mind as much causing their skills to weaken.

BE AWARE OF THE COMPANY THAT YOU KEEP

FOR YOUR COMPANY CAN EITHER SHARPEN

OR DULLEN YOUR SHARPNESS

=Tre Nitty Gritty=

TOOL # 48

LEAD BY EXAMPLE

AS A LEADER, IT IS YOUR RESPONSIBILITY

TO TEACH YOUR FOLLOWERS

HOW TO BECOME GREAT LEADERS

One of the most important and effective aspects to Think Rich / Live rich is to lead by example for seeing is believing. Not only do you have to Think Rich, Live Rich and spread those riches but you must also practice what you preach. Imagine someone rambling on and on talking your ears off bragging and boasting about how much money they are set out to make and displaying all of their plans to the public but they are so busy talking about it that they tire themselves out and fail to get anything accomplished.

Then think of the one who rarely speaks of their plans and instead is more active at bringing them into existence. With this, you are able to bear witness to their success with your own eyes and take it as being fact for the reason that seeing is believing. Some people talk so much that they end up actually not saying anything at all, while others say less and accomplish more with fewer words. Saying nothing says a lot so say less and do more.

Being a leader is a full-time job. Having the opportunity to lead is something to be honored and appreciated. Honored and appreciated. This is something that's not to be taken lightly for you as a leader can either lead your followers off of a cliff or to open doors of opportunity that will lead them to success. Do not be a misleader... Be a positive influence.

Avoid telling people to steer clear of a particular thing, yet allow yourself to succumb to whatever it is that you insist should be refrained from. You will be viewed as a person of contradictory practice, discrediting your leadership. You will begin to be looked at as someone who is not one to lead by example. Instead of practicing what you preach you are preaching without practicing.

Take full responsibility for your position and strive to be the best leader that you possibly can because your life is not the only one at stake. As a leader you are responsible for the lives of others. You have their futures resting in the palms of your hands and what's to come all depends on your leadership skills... Teach prosperity and show others how to become preposterous.

Spread your wealth and teach others how to become wealthy. Explain how SELF WEALTH is the first step towards acquiring FINANCIAL WEALTH. Just as you can't fully love or respect anyone else until you fully love and respect yourself. In order for you to become financially stable you will first have to become stable in your state of existence. Once you become in-tune with these things it will assist you with becoming a better leader. With that, you will be able to teach your followers how to become better leaders by LEADING BY EXAMPLE.

TOOL # 49

BUILD YOUR TEAM

BUILD YOUR TEAM ON A SOLID FOUNDATION

OF MORALS AND PRINCIPALS

IN DOING THIS YOU WILL CREATE

A CIRCLE OF POWER

=Tre Nitty Gritty=

Building your team is an important task that should be taken very seriously. You need to know that YOUR TEAM MATTERS... As a rich thinker you will have to be able to recognize an individual's abilities in order to be able to place them into the proper positions. Sit down and interview individuals on an individual basis in order to become familiar with their strengths as well as their flawed areas. This process will play a part in how well your vehicle will function.

As long as every piece works in harmony the chemistry will be aligned to perfection and the results will be astronomical. If you do not know this by now you should let it soak into your memory and lock it in. One bad apple can spoil the bunch just as one small leak can cause a ship to sink. You do not want people who carry negative energy around, to take a seat at your table or even have a space in your presence. This will only bring disorder where there should be order and structure.

You have to take it upon yourself to weed out the bad seeds for they will only do what they do and that is... Breed corruption. The goal of a team is to work in unison in order to achieve a particular goal. This is something that can happen very smoothly or it can become a very complicated task if your team is busy not being a team.

Building your team should be just as important if not more important to you as putting together a plan followed up with a plan of action being that the team is what it will take to work that plan and make sure that it operates and functions to its full potential.

Your team can be built with people from different areas in your life whether it be your family, friends, associates, affiliates or whatever label you choose to place upon the ones who surround you. A team's purpose is to come together and stick together. Valuing one another's ideas, sharing a similar vision or interest and making advancements as a collective unit.

A team should represent togetherness... You will have to choose your teammates wisely. This can be in reference to a significant other that you may meet and begin to grow close to. As you begin to learn about someone, signs and symbols will let you know if the two of you are compatible.

Ask yourself... Do the two of us have similar goals, or any goals at all? Maybe one has goals and the other doesn't. Do you value each other's opinions? suggestions? Support one another or have the ability to build and create great things together?

One major sign that you must pay complete attention to in all aspects is if there is a tilt on the scale of responsibility that causes an off-set of balance. You do not want to find yourself being the bearer of all things and having to pull the weight for your other team members. If they aren't playing their part, then of what use are they?

If you are having to carry your entire team on your back, it would only make sense to lighten up the load by cutting loose and letting go of dead weight, replacing it with strength and building muscle that will assist you with continuing to move forward while continuing to make forward progression. Your team should make things run smoother not make things more complicated.

If you cannot hold a meeting or gathering where people will wait patiently and take their turns speaking, voicing their opinions in a respectful and organized manner... This is not a good representation of how teamwork works. Strive for respect and order over disrespect and disorder.

Your TEAM VALUES will have to be instilled into your teammates. Not one member should have the mindset that they are more or less important than the next member. We all have to know to appreciate and respect one another's position. Don't be mad because he or she is the Boss... Recognize and respect their position as being the Boss, play your position, monitor their moves, Boss up and become a Boss yourself.

YOU CAN'T FULLY PLAY YOUR POSITION

WHILE PAYING TOO MUCH ATTENTION

TO SOMEONE ELSE'S STATUS

=Tre Nitty Gritty=

TOOL # 50

USE YOUR TOOLS

HAVING A COLLECTION OF TOOLS

THAT YOU DO NOT USE

IS NOT FOR THE WISE MINDED

=Tre Nitty Gritty=

Think Rich / Live Rich is a combination of universal tools... A formula that was developed to be applied to one's life. There is no particular order that you must follow with this process, the most important rule is that you USE YOUR TOOLS.

Do not become a collector of these valuable assets and not USE them to add value to your life. We all have a mission, a purpose, a reason for being. The tools of Think Rich / Live Rich are here to open the eyes and minds of all individuals assisting them with finding the rich inner-being that resides within them.

Cleanse the mind... There is a need to have a cleansed mind and a clear vision in order to operate effectively. Once you have cleansed your mind, using your tools should become your primary focus. Have Rich Self Talk, take the time to communicate with yourself. Assess your situation, come up with solutions and motivate yourself to do great things.

Be thankful for all things in life because all things in life are a blessing whether it be good or bad. You just have to TRAIN YOUR BRAIN to see things this way. You have to Get Active / Stay Active, remain physically and mentally fit for the two of them to work interchangeably. Exercising your body also exercises your mind just as exercising your mind will work wonders for your existence.

Reprogram yourself by erasing all negative teachings, thoughts, behaviors etc. Seek and acquire fruitful knowledge that will assist you with becoming the RICH YOU. Do your own thinking instead of allowing others to do the thinking for you. By taking control of your thoughts, you will take control of your actions and with taking control of your actions you will take control of your life.

Troubleshooting will assist you with recognizing your trouble areas that are in need of fixing. Address your flaws, repair them and keep them polished. Power Thinking is a Power Tool that has the ability of drilling, hammering, destructing, demolishing, re-constructing and re-building your thoughts, coming up with extraordinary goals to accomplish and a plan to achieve them.

Communication is a must have in the land of signs, symbols and conversation. Use your communication skills for everything that they are worth and communicate your way to success. You must have patience being that everything takes time to come into existence... That's just a law of human nature. At times we all may become anxious, restless and eager to get things done but like the saying goes... Good things come to those who wait.

Your observance is very important... You have to be mindful of the people, places and things that you subject yourself to. It could mean the difference between life or death, success or failure, profit or loss. To be aware is to be alive so master being observant. Boss up and be your own boss whether you are a BOSS or a WORKER. Boss yourself around and do not allow yourself to become content. Always strive for improvement, build your own business and become your own brand.

Avoid blood suckers and dream killers for they will attempt to knock you down, kick you while you are down and prevent you from getting back up to your feet. They will suck all of life out of you along with your dreams so be sure to keep your distance from them at all cost. Stay in your own lane and march to the beat of your own drum. What someone else eats won't satisfy your hunger. Do what you do and do it the best... Put your all into it then put some more into it. Ride your own wave and stay in your own lane.

When it comes to growth, this is a process that has a need to be continuous. So, do not stop growing for the moment that you are no longer living. You are simply alive and breathing. The minute that you stop growing is the second that you will begin dying. You have to Evolve, expand, elevate and continue growing by all means necessary. Preparation is a mandatory tool that is needed in all aspects of life. If you stay ready you won't have to get ready so stay prepared.

Live the dream instead of dreaming the dream for as long as you are dreaming it is only an illusion. The moment that you begin living the dream it is in existence. No Days Off is something that separates the determined and the motivated from the content and the stagnant. Take breaks when they are called for but 24 hours is too long to go without getting SOMETHING done. Make your days count because tomorrow isn't promised to any of us.

Every dollar counts whether you are doing addition, subtraction, multiplication or division. It all comes back to its original origin of NUMBERS that are to be calculated and accounted for because every dollar counts all the way down to the penny. Use your money as leverage... Do not become a slave who works for money, make money become your slave and make it work for you.

Balance is a law of nature... The earth rotates and sits at a certain degree of balance as with anything else that stands in the universe. The laws of gravity assist us with balancing ourselves. It is up to us to balance our minds, bodies, souls and keep them steady.

You have to Think outside the box... Do not continue to be confined by walls and barriers or allow roadblocks, turmoil, tragedy, trials and tribulations to keep you boxed in. Some may tell you that there is no way out of a particular situation, planting this negative seed into our brain... But who are they, to do YOUR THINKING for YOU? Keep searching for a way out... you have to think outside of the box in order to escape the box.

Build bridges and do not burn them... You never know when you may need to return to and or depend on a person, place or a particular thing. So, strive to stay in good grace and continue to build new bridges, make new connections and create new opportunities for the bigger your NETWORK the bigger your SAFETY NET.

Quality and Quantity is important for the fact that there is a need for the two of them to coexist alongside one another. You want to have a quantity of good qualities as a human being. With this you will have the ability of providing a quantity of quality work, services and or product.

Embrace losses being that they will become a part of your success story. Turn every loss into a lesson then count them as a blessing for without losses there would be no wins.

Monitor your progress on a regular basis. This will keep you aware of your current position from the distance that you have come while assisting you with developing a plan to get where you are going. Multi-focusing is a skill of multitasking. You have to have the ability to focus on multiple things at once. In doing this you will be able to accomplish a lot of things at one time using a particular science and whatever unique strategy that works for you. Your dedication will determine whether or not you will proceed towards reaching your goal or become frustrated and give up before your mission is complete. Stay dedicated and determined for your dedication will drive you to your destination.

Resilience is a master tool of survival... You have to have the ability to bend and alter your shape or appearance to fit into any situation in order to come out unscathed and revert back to your original form unaffected by the occurrence. In a world filled with adversity it is imperative that we have resilience and know how and when to be resilient.

Learn to benefit in all that you do for if it's not beneficial then it is not useful. Time is valuable, utilize every second for what they are worth. You have to remain humble throughout every level of life that you experience whether it's when you are at the bottom of the bottom or at the tip of the top. Humbleness will keep you afloat through deadly waters and hurricanes.

Continuing to evolve is simply another form of growth. If you do not evolve you will remain stuck in your ways, thoughts and position in life. Change is good as long as that change is for the better. You must first conquer your fears in order to conquer the world. If you allow your nervousness to prevent you from making a decision, it may prevent you from elevating to a height that you never imagined all because you had a fear that you failed to conquer.

Strive to capitalize off of everything that you possibly can. Any book that you read, find the meat inside of the shell and devour it. Any music that you listen to or television that you watch, find a message that lies within. Take advantage of opportunities and capitalize in life all around the board.

We all have scars and the only way to recover from them is with our own self-healing... When no outside force can assist us with what's going on inside of us, we will have to dig deep and heal ourselves. Find your motivation and do what motivates you. This in many ways could motivate others to find their motivation and you will be living out the purpose of Think Rich / Live Rich. The main thing is finding what works for you and working with it.

Prioritize your life, for a life without organization is unorganized. If you do not have your priorities in order, you will not know what things are most important in order for you to be able to put first things first and handle your priorities in a prioritized fashion. Express yourself and let it be known what it is that you stand for. Demand respect but show respect in order to receive it.

True consistency is a function that is founded and established by our habits. Being consistent is the mark of the champion so earn your championship through your consistency. Effective thinking is a process of having effective, positive thoughts that breeds Rich results. Do not waste your time wrestling around with frivolous thinking that will in no way have a positive impact on your life.

Morals and principles are characteristic laws to live by and stand upon. Lacking these will hinder your life. Hold on to your integrity... your soul depends on it. Confidence can either make or break you. It can either pull you into or keep you away from reaching your goals and dreams. Have enough courage and confidence to know that you have the ability to move mountains.

Sacrificing is something that we all will come to face at some point in time or another. We will have to let go of certain things in order to have the ability to grab ahold of something of richer value. It's all about having enough common sense to know when and what to sacrifice. You must also live and learn along the way. Do not just go through life ignoring the lessons that life provides us. Make sure that you continue seeking to learn as much as possible. When you live, learn and bring the two of them together the results will be monumental.

Planning your actions without planning is foolish. The more that you plan, the more direct your impact will become... If you fail to plan, you plan to fail so be sure to plan your action. Open Eyes will open doors. Your sight and vision is a tool that must be utilized to its full potential, so use your eyes as your guide to see the doors of opportunity and open them.

Being broke vs being broken are two completely different things. Having the ability to take notice and knowing the difference between the two can save you a lot of time and energy when dealing with people in the world. Something or someone that is broken financially can be fixed but something or someone that is broken and destroyed beyond repair is an entirely different complex Delima.

Master your emotions, do not allow your emotions to master you. Your emotions can either take you to a dark place or lead you to a bright and beautiful one. Become the driver of your emotions and master the energy that circulates throughout your body. Steel sharpens steel, just as we have the ability to sharpen each other as a people. Continue to build with others and sharpen each other's tools by exchanging information that will sharpen the mind.

Lead by example... Do not become one who does not practice what they preach for this would make you out to be a hypocrite. Show and prove... Show others the way and give them the tools that they need to become a great leader who leads by example. Build your team and teach them how to be a team... Show them the difference in the results of teamwork and being on one accord compared to being unorganized and divided.

Something that I cannot stress enough and I feel is the most important tool of them all and that is that you USE YOUR TOOLS... Think Rich / Live Rich and become the RICH YOU!

ABOUT THE AUTHOR

Tre nitty Gritty is an inspirational author who intends to uplift the universe with the universal tools of Think Rich / Live Rich. Born and raised in Waterloo, Iowa... A place that has been deemed by "Wall Street 24/7" as the most dangerous city and the worst place to live being of African American descent. Stating that the chances of surviving are slim to none and the possibility of flourishing into a successful individual being next to impossible due to the lack of resources and opportunities.

Growing up, Tre Nitty Gritty was exposed to gangs, violence, drugs, drug dealers and drug users. With that... Venturing off into a lifestyle of criminal activity was simply a thing of the norm. During his early teenage years... Tre Nitty Gritty became a product of his environment. In doing so, his wrong decision making has cost him and led him to serve multiple stints in prison serving time in both federal and Iowa state prisons for guns and drug related charges.

On a quest of bettering himself and making some positive changes, Tre Nitty Gritty has developed the system of Think Rich / Live Rich, applied it to his life and has become his RICH SELF... Ultimately, instead of continuing to be a part of the problem, he has now become a part of the solution by providing a formula for positive growth and rich development. After falling victim and becoming a product of his environment Tre Nitty Gritty is now striving to make his environment become a product of the new individual that he has now become.

With Think Rich / Live Rich, Tre Nitty Gritty has made the transition from living a life of crime to living a life of prosperity. From a life of being in and out of confinement to having his feet planted firm on RICH SOIL as a writer, teacher, music producer / engineer, Hip Hop / Rap artist, Screen-play writer, actor, director, consultant, motivational speaker, inspirational leader, life coach, advisor, community activist, reliable and responsible adult, man, son, parent, brother, friend and all-around business man.

Tre Nitty Gritty is the CEO of TRE NITTY GRITTY INCORPORATED... That stands as the parent company over a slew of subsidiary LLC companies such as TNG FILMS,

C-Y-I-$ELL MUSIC,   O's & POUNDS PRODUCTIONS etc... Follow and keep up with the latest from Tre Nitty Gritty.

WISE WORDS FROM TRE NITTY GRITTY

I began bossing myself around, built my own business and became my own brand... Think Rich / Live Rich and you too can become the RICH YOU!

HOW TO USE THIS BOOK

READ, DISSECT, DIGEST, REGURGITATE

READ: Interpret mentally, look for or find hidden messages and meanings. Decode, study, come to understand.

DISSECT: Cut into pieces, examine, analyze.

DIGEST: Think over, convert (food) into a form that can be absorbed, summarize.

REGURGITATE: Vomit (release back into the atmosphere) Environment, cast or pour out again.

=Sneek= Jamell Rouson # 005514-027 www.bop.gov

Made in the USA
Columbia, SC
18 September 2022

67261429R00054